Canadians:
Seriously
Humorous

Candid comments, quips and quotes

compiled by

Mervin R. Hempel

Order this book online at www.trafford.com/07-2023
or email orders@trafford.com

Most Trafford titles are also available at major online book retailers.

© Copyright 2009 Mervin R. Hempel.

All rights reserved. No part of this publication may be reproduced, stored in a retrieval system, or transmitted, in any form or by any means, electronic, mechanical, photocopying, recording, or otherwise, without the written prior permission of the author.

Every effort was made to determine whether previously published material included in this book required permission to reprint. If there has been any error or inadvertent omission on the part of the author, he apologizes and a correction will be made in any subsequent editions.

Design and Illustration: Mavis Andrews
Cover art/illustrations © Copyright 2009 Mavis Andrews
http://peavi.bc.ca/members/MavisAndrews.html

Note for Librarians: A cataloguing record for this book is available from Library and Archives Canada at www.collectionscanada.ca/amicus/index-e.html

Printed in Victoria, BC, Canada.

ISBN: 978-1-4251-4715-0

We at Trafford believe that it is the responsibility of us all, as both individuals and corporations, to make choices that are environmentally and socially sound. You, in turn, are supporting this responsible conduct each time you purchase a Trafford book, or make use of our publishing services. To find out how you are helping, please visit www.trafford.com/responsiblepublishing.html

Our mission is to efficiently provide the world's finest, most comprehensive book publishing service, enabling every author to experience success. To find out how to publish your book, your way, and have it available worldwide, visit us online at www.trafford.com/10510

www.trafford.com

North America & international
toll-free: 1 888 232 4444 (USA & Canada)
phone: 250 383 6864 ♦ fax: 250 383 6804
email: info@trafford.com

The United Kingdom & Europe
phone: +44 (0)1865 487 395 ♦ local rate: 0845 230 9601
facsimile: +44 (0)1865 481 507 ♦ email: info.uk@trafford.com

10 9 8 7 6 5 4 3 2 1

Canadians: Seriously Humorous

Candid comments, quips and quotes

compiled by

Mervin R. Hempel

Printed in Canada

© Copyright 2009 Mervin R. Hempel

All rights reserved. No part of this publication may be reproduced, stored in a retrieval system, or transmitted, in any form or by any means, electronic, mechanical, photocopying, recording, or otherwise, without the written prior permission of the author.

Every effort was made to determine whether previously published material included in this book required permission to reprint. If there has been any error or inadvertent omission on the part of the author, he apologizes and a correction will be made in any subsequent editions.

Design and Illustration: Mavis Andrews
Cover art/illustrations © Copyright 2009 Mavis Andrews
http://peavi.bc.ca/members/MavisAndrews.html

Note for Librarians: A cataloguing record for this book is available from Library and Archives Canada at: www.collectionscanada.ca/amicus/index-e.html
Printed in Victoria, BC, Canada

ISBN 978-1-4251-4715-0

Order this book online at www.trafford.com/07-2023
or email: orders@trafford.com

www.trafford.com
North America & international
toll-free: 1 888 232 4444 (USA & Canada)
phone: 250 383 6864 fax: 250 383 6804
email: info@trafford.com
The United Kingdom & Europe
phone: +44 (0)1865 722 113 local rate: 0845 230 9601
facsimile: +44 (0)1865 722 868 email: info.uk@trafford.com
10 9 8 7 6 5 4 3 2 1

Contents

Foreword 1

Canada—From Coast to Coast 5
   Canada (General) 6
   Toronto 10
   Sudbury 11
   Edmonton 11
   Calgary 12
   Regina 12
   Montreal 12
   Victoria 13
   New Minas 14
   Halifax 14
   Kingston 14
   Ottawa 14
   Kitchener 15
   Vancouver 15
   Winnipeg 16
   Newfoundland 16
   Saskatchewan 17
   Manitoba 18
   Alberta 18
   Quebec 19
   Ontario 19
   British Columbia 19
   Nova Scotia 20

Way Too Much Geography—Regions 21
- Regions (General) 22
- The North 23
- East Vs. West 26

The People—Who We Are 28
- The People (General) 29
- Women 33
- Men 38
- Farmers 39

Getting Around & Communicating 40
- The Railway 41
- The Media 43

Politics and Government 45
- Politics (General) 46
- Politicians and Political Parties 47
- Patronage 48
- Politicians 49
- House of Commons 50
- Senate 51
- Intellectuals 52
- Federal Budget 52
- New Democratic Party 53
- Liberals 54
- Conservatives 55
- Civil Servants 57
- RCMP 58
- Armed Forces 59

Them and Us 61
- Social Class & Status 62

Economics 63
Banks 66
The Law 67
The Foreign Connection 70

The Environment 76
Pollution 77
Fresh Air 78

You Call that Culture? 79
Culture (General) 80
Health 83
Labour 84
Education 85
The Language 85
Bilingualism 86
French Language 87
English Language 88
Sex 89
Food and Drink 90
Art and Literature 93
Miscellaneous 97

For the Love of Sports 100
Sports (General) 101
Golf 102
Football 103
Baseball 104
Hockey 104

Odds & Ends and Leftovers 108
Odds & Ends 109
Leftovers 110

Acknowledgements

I am happy to express my appreciation to a number of people who helped me while writing and compiling this book. First and foremost is my wife, Judith, who was always supportive over the years that it took to finally get this book to print. Also, to our two grown children, Brad and Jennifer, who weren't born when this book was first hatched.

To my good friends and golfing buddies, Tom Beggs and John Fahey, who made it so much fun to discuss the possibilities of the book.

To my proofreaders, Roger Mitchell and Lynn Byrnell, for catching typos and errors. And, last but not least, to my patient editor and designer, Mavis Andrews, who was always available for fresh ideas and support.

Many thanks to you all.

Foreword

SO, I'M AT this fundraiser put on by the then Australian Prime Minister and his party. I won't say which party it was—it might affect book sales.

Anyway, the Prime Minister is there doing what he does best: raising funds for the election campaign and telling one-liners that every journalist drools at the thought of getting for inclusion in tomorrow's newspapers. Wherever I was at that event, there he was, with his people, encouraging me to give to the party coffers. He must have thought that I was a rich former Canadian, establishing his roots in

Aussie Land and looking for something to support (other than what was used when I played soccer). Well, I didn't have the heart to tell him I wasn't rich and that my contribution to the cause wouldn't even be enough to pay for all the tea and scones I was enjoying at the party. Tagging behind me, at my every step, was this fine-looking young lady who was also enjoying the free goodies, and who kept bothering me with hurried speech, saying, "Have I got an idea for you..." But I'm thinking to myself, "Not now, dear."

All right then, so it didn't happen quite that way.

How the idea for my first book came about was slightly different. I was in Sydney, Australia, but it was at a book signing in a bookstore. At least that part of the above story isn't phony (along with the fine-looking young lady, who happened to be my new bride). I'd like to tell you that the guest of honour was someone famous, but I left all my lies back in the first paragraph. My new bride, thinking that I could write anything that people would want to read (silly her), suggested in a low voice, "I know what your first book should be! You should collect humorous put-downs about Canada and Canadians and compile them into a book. Some Aussie writer recently wrote a similar book," she said, "only about Australia and Australians, I believe. I picked it up and flipped through it in the bookstore here, and it really was funny."

Well, all that happened about thirty-some years ago, when my wife and I were newly married, after we had decided to hop aboard a ship and sail to Down Under for new experiences in a new land; new to us anyway. This book truly has been some thirty years in the making, and now here it is, in your hot little hands. I hope you paid for it before you opened it up—I haven't paid my editor yet and I need the money.

I thought my wife's idea was marvellous. Such a book would be a great first book to tackle. In fact, I was so excited about the prospect that I forgot to buy the Aussie version of the book. I had to hop a bus and head back to the bookstore, track down that book and purchase it for $2.50 Australian. A bus? I told you I wasn't rich. (Oops, that's another statement that isn't phony.)

Did I mention that both my wife and I are Canadians? Yes sir,

FOREWORD

Canadians all our lives. After three glorious years of working and touring around Australia, I really began to miss the grub at my favourite hot dog stand, and so we moved back to Canada, our homeland.

My wife and I have travelled extensively in Canada since our time in Australia, speaking with many hundreds of people, as one might expect. However, they all had nothing to do with putting this book together or contributing quotes. Maybe their quotes weren't humorous enough, or maybe I just didn't bother to write down what they said. The quotes in this book come from many different sources, many from Canadian newspapers such as *The Globe and Mail*, *The Red Deer Advocate*, and the *Victoria Times Colonist*, as well as magazines such as *Maclean's*. I have not used television or the Internet, to the best of my knowledge, as sources for quotes. The somewhat serious and informative introduction to each section provides a fresh background, a perspective on the reality of Canada and Canadians. A couple of somewhat serious quotes may even have found their way onto a page or two.

This book is essentially a one-person production. Expect the unexpected! If there are any errors of omission or commission, or if a particularly unkind put-down in the form of a quote or within other material in this book offends anyone, then let me know, as such matters drawn to my attention may be immediately omitted from future printings.

I have to say, I am truly sorry that I have not been able to put down, in some humorous way, every city, town, village, or every interesting and well-known or not-so-well-known person in Canada. As you can probably understand, after thirty-some years of collecting quotes, I am hamstrung by such annoying limitations as time, space, and interest. Of course, you could send me some insultingly humorous things to say about your own hometown, or whatever, and (if it makes me laugh), it may be included in a revised edition to be written sometime in the next thirty years—if I'm lucky enough to live that long. I wanted to include lots of pictures to enhance the humour, but could not since the cost of illustrations is borne 100 percent by the author. So, I decided to go the cheaper way with a relatively unadorned, basically bland, almost understated look to the book without a whole bunch of pictures to distract you from all the serious introductions to the sections and humorous quotations that surely will tickle your funny bone. I know you don't mind this. After all, you bought the book, and for that I am grateful. Did I mention that I wasn't rich?

Canada—From Coast to Coast

WE CANNOT FULLY begin to understand the ways of a man unless we fully study the environment of which he is a part. This book, therefore, begins with the vast land mass that is called Canada—a land of great extremes of climate and terrain, and great distances from shore to shore. The remoteness of Canada from the Old World, its nearness to the United States, and the hardships that it inflicts upon those who inhabit it, shape the characters and attitudes of its inhabitants more than we know or may care to admit.

Canada (General)

Canada is a "great white waste of time" whose "docile, Zamboni-driving" Molson-sucking citizens consume seal casseroles as they export terrorism, mad cow disease "and even deadlier Gordon Lightfoot and Nickelback albums" to the United States, American media reports last week.

Cristin Schmitz, CanWest News Service,
The Province, March 28, 2005

It's so cold in Canada that as early as October, the pizzerias have to change to winter-weight olive oil.

Robert Shelly, 1976

Canada was built on dead beavers.

Margaret Atwood, author, Arts Report,
National Public Radio, September 19, 1988

Give Yanks a Taste of Their Own Medicine:
I was laughing out loud at the *New York Times*' shots aimed at Canada. "It's true, so true," I giggled between paragraphs. "I'd kill for a seal casserole right now."
Anyone offended or disappointed by the jabs needs to shake it off, suck it up and...well, retaliate.
So let's set our pens to stun and take some friendly shots back at their flag-wavin', Big-Mac eatin', oil-baron-votin', steroid-takin', atomic-bomb-inventin', wild-goose-terrorist-chasin' butts. After all, what's a little smack-talking between allies?

Jakob Zaiss, Mill Bay, BC,
Times Colonist, March 30, 2005

Much will have to change in Canada if the country is to stay the same.

Abraham Rotstein, 1965

Canada is a collection of ten provinces with strong governments loosely connected by fear.
> *Dave Broadfoot, television comedian, paraphrased by G. Clark in* Canada: The Uneasy Neighbour, *1965*

"This is unfortunate for Canada," read the straight-faced report, "where so many men are needed to open up the virgin parts of the country."
> *The Daily Mirror, London, England*

Corruption pervades every tissue of our society.
> *Sir Wilfrid Laurier, letter to Blake, December 7, 1881*

A number of U.S. publications have proclaimed recently that Canada is cool. We sat out the Iraq war, we let same-sex couples smoke dope at their wedding receptions, we have cheap medicines—yes, sir, we here in the Great White North are hip, we're with it, we're happenin' dudes.

Or not. It's also true Canadians go to the U.S. for medical care, we're overtaxed, we couldn't outfight Andorra, and the marijuana and gay-marriage issues divide Canadians sharply. One man's cool, we're afraid, is another man's strung out.
> *The Gazette, Montreal, October 2003*

The symbol of Canada is the beaver, the industrious rodent whose destiny it was to furnish hats that warmed better brains than his own.
> *Roy Daniells, 1957*

Sure, "Keep it Canadian."
But how? You know, who do we push around?
> *Pierre E. Trudeau to the Press after meeting with a delegation from the Committee for an Independent Canada, June 29, 1971*

Would you like to know a secret? Here it is! There is a second Trans-Canada Highway from north to south just like the one from east to west. Nobody knows about it but it runs all the way from the American border to the Arctic Ocean. We know it's there but we have not pieced it together in our minds because the federal government does not want us to think of it as a Trans-Canada Highway.

Brian Brown, 1978

Canada is a country whose major problems are never solved.

A.R.M. Lower, 1967

An official report on accidents in Canada revealed that twice as many men as women are killed.

The Daily Mirror, *London, England, date unknown*

President Richard Nixon said, "I am not a crook." Then there was the U.S. president who said, "I did not have sex with that woman." Now, the B.C. finance minister says we have no money [and] everyone has to cut back. Then, the year before the election, a miracle occurs and money rains from the sky and everyone cheers.

Bob Riche, Qualicum Beach

It is outrageous to imply that our beloved provincial government [British Columbia] is associated with organized crime.

There is nothing at all organized about this government.

If they were put in charge of organizing crime, based on how well they have run everything else, the following might occur: the streets would be safe, the police would be out of work, the jails would be empty—and could be sold off with the rest of our assets.

Bob Cameron, January 13, 2004

Feller Citizens, this country is goin' to the dogs hand over hand.

T.C. Haliburton, Sam Slick, *1836*

The typical Canadian, if such a creature can be described, is an employee who makes less than one-third as much as the typical M.P. and she's female, since there are more women than men in this country.

Don McGillivray, Calgary Herald, *January 2, 1985*

I wish to extend a humble invitation to the people in the east to come to Banff while you can still afford to enter the National Park and there are still a few trees left standing within the town.

We've got four lanes of highway, flyovers and cloverleafs, massive concrete mountaintop reservoirs and a new parking lot that would do the C.N.E. proud. So bring lots of film and take lots of photos of Parks Canada concrete. If you're lucky, there may be a few trees remaining. This nation's legacy, indeed!

Paul Lake, Banff, Alberta, 1984

Fuddle Duddle: Euphemism for go to hell; drop dead.

Origin: what Prime Minister Pierre Trudeau claimed he said in Parliament rather than a profanity.

Katherine Barber, Only in Canada, You Say, *2007*

Canadians tend to feel someone's minding the shop. Though they've had access to American know-how, British political wisdom and French Culture, Canadians have managed to end up with British know-how, French political wisdom and American culture.

Jeanette Harris, 1976

For Canada is frighteningly bureaucratic. The Archetypal Canadian, at God's right hand when He created heaven and earth, advised Him to work through a committee.

Dennis Duffy, 1979

Don't smile—you're Canadian.

Elizabeth Thompson,
CanWest News Service, August 2003

"Why work?" he joked, noting the size of the crowd on a weekday afternoon. "Free health care, right?"

Jason Chow, February 11, 2004

If a pig had his rights, he would be our national emblem, instead of the beaver. What has the beaver done for us, anyway? The pig, on the other hand, sustained our fathers in their fight against the wilderness, and yet his name is a name of scorn.

Peter McArthur, 1915

Canadians are in truth a prosaic people. A candid historian of the American Revolution terms them a "tamer, less inventive people" who have never shown power of initiative like the colonists who make the United States.

Archibald MacMechan, 1974

If two Canadians understand snow they are then both Canadians.
  If one Canadian understands snow and another doesn't understand snow at all, then one is a Canadian and the other is no Canadian at all.

Carl Sandburg, 1928

Toronto

On watching Torontonians eating ice-cream cones:
  The spectacle which hit me most forcefully on a sunny Sunday afternoon was that of the enormous number of adults who were engaged as ruminatively as any cud-chewing cow, in the operation of licking ice-cream cones.

McKenzie Porter, in a column in the
Toronto Telegram, July 26, 1965

First prize, one week in Toronto.
Second prize, two weeks in Toronto.

Old Canadian saying

Hogtown (so called because outsiders accused Torontonians of taking everything unto themselves):
So I don't really know about Canada. My roots are in Toronto: all but six months of my married life here, my children all born here, my closest friends here, my first and only career job here. What's Canadian about these roots? You know how Toronto is: if they A-bombed it, they wouldn't kill a single Canadian (so I've heard a dozen Canadians say).

Dennis Duffy, 1979

Toronto is still a cold city to me—and I'm not talking about the weather. I got off the train this morning and asked the directions. No one would answer me. Is this Toronto's hospitality?

The Toronto Star, *November 24, 1956*

Sudbury

But "only God can make a tree."
He'll never try it in Sudbury.

Raymond Souster, 1979

Edmonton

He is a well-balanced Edmontonian, he has a chip on BOTH shoulders.

Bruce Hanley, 2001

Calgary

There can be nothing more ludicrous than a grown man with a paunch teetering around Calgary on the high heels and pointed toes of cowboy boots, attempting to capture some primitive cachet from some distant past.

Allan Fotheringham, columnist,
Fictionary of Facts and Follies, 2001

For the first time Toronto was eclipsed by another city as the butt of bad jokes—"The city we love to hate"—Calgary.

John Robert Colombo, 1983

Calgary is Alberta.

Oh, I know that the capital of the Province is in Edmonton but who the hell wants to go all that way north when you can meet the same kind of people 200 miles to the south.

Ben Wicks, 1976

Regina

"The site of Regina is flat," as Sir John A. Macdonald noted on his visit in 1886: "If you had a lit-tle more wood, and a lit-tle more water, and here and there a hill, I think the prospect would be improved.

John Robert Colombo, 1983

Montreal

Montreal is rotten to the core, and if all Canada be like it, the sooner we have done with it, the better.

Lord Elgin, April 25, 1849

Montreal is riot-prone; I'm sorry, but there it is. Racial and religious strife, labour troubles, French nationalism, English pig-headedness, strong and opposing views on the merits of conscription during the two world wars—all of these added to the troubles that accrue to any large city have to keep the place in ferment for centuries.
Walter Stewart, 1976

Victoria

Victoria is God's waiting room. It is the only cemetery in the entire world with street lighting.
Anon., 1972

Another reason we [Victorians] don't belong in Canada:
  Driving tests were cancelled this week, due to unsafe conditions on side streets. Local teenagers, eager for that big green "N," cursed their bad luck. Real Canadians, however, insist their teens pass driving tests on the most slippery nights, so they can send them out to pick up videos, no matter how awful the weather.
Vivian Smith, January 11, 2004

We never turned anyone down. I listened to lunatic after lunatic.
Peter Pollen, on his willingness to hear from the public when he was Victoria's mayor,
Times Colonist, *October 18, 2006*

With its manicured trees, fish and chip houses, and 19th century façades, the only thing missing from the Englishness of Victoria is a Rent-A-Corgi service.
Tyee Bridge

I thought it was Jurassic Park or something!
Brent Butt, on Victoria's aging population,
Times Colonist, *November 4, 2006*

New Minas

And The Crappiest Town is…"Like Excrement":
Readers Pick Nova Scotia Town to Dump On.
Kerry Underwood,
New Minas, NS, April 6, 2004

Halifax

Halifax is a peculiar town; the wooden houses all look alike. The people are somewhat grim, little inclined to be facetious.
Solange Chaput Rolland, 1966

Hell or Halifax:
The alternative destination of the United Empire Loyalists on their expulsion from New England, about 1783.
Anon., 1983

Kingston

Indeed, it may be said of Kingston, that one half of it appears to be burnt down, and the other half not to be built up.
Charles Dickens, American Notes, *1842*

Ottawa

The secret to having a good time in Ottawa? Move.
Will Ferguson and Ian Ferguson,
How To Be A Canadian, *2007*

The Westminster in the Wilderness.

Anon., 1858

Ottawa? Well, it is sort of a provincial Washington. That's it. Yesterday's city tomorrow!

Allan Fotheringham, 1972

Kitchener

Kitchener was called Sand Hill and Ebytown before it was named Berlin in 1824 in deference to its Pennsylvania Dutch settlers from Pennsylvania and immigrants from Germany.

In 1916, the name was changed to honour the British war leader, the late Lord Kitchener of Khartoum.

John Robert Colombo, 1983

Vancouver

Where else could a loudmouth like me win an election except in a crazy city like this?

Tom Campbell, Mayor, quoted in
Maclean's, *August 1967*

It is a city that should have grown straight up, like Manhattan, instead of despoiling great mountainsides and blotching fair valleys.

Edward McCourt, 1965

They get so much rain in Vancouver that they don't tan. They rust.

Anon.,
a former Vancouverite

Winnipeg

We're a hundred dollars from anywhere.
Anon., a popular saying,
Winnipeg, late nineteenth century

The windiest intersection in all of Canada is said to be Portage and Main in downtown Winnipeg. Here, the story goes, the prevailing winds over the last forty years have shifted the entire intersection six inches to the west.
John Robert Colombo, 1983

But it is for natives only. Not many Canadians are strong enough to sustain its climate or its pace. Why, there were winter mornings when I walked half a mile to the Free Press office in an advanced state of rigor mortis, and I have sat all day in a cold bath when the wind came in blowtorch blast from the south.
Bruce Hutchinson in
Canada: Tomorrow's Giant, *1957*

I wouldn't say it's cold, but every year Winnipeg's athlete of the year is an ice fisherman.
Dale Tallon, U.S. journalist,
in Sports Illustrated, *December 22, 1986*

Newfoundland

False Girdle? Newfoundland place name.

The island is ruled by King Joseph the First of Smallwood, whose twin brother, Prince Jean of Drapeau, rules the principality of Montreal.
Ben Wicks, 1976

The only reason Newfie jokes are so simple is because we want mainlanders to understand them.

William Kurelek, 1975

"Confederation!" he saluted above the wind. "Why, Confederation was the bloodiest fool thing we ever did. The new industries? They'll all go broke, you'll see, and when de Americans finish spendin' money on de air fields, Newf'nland'll be finished too." He laughed bitterly and added for my benefit: "Then Canada can take care of us."

A Newfoundlander, in Bruce Hutchinson's
Canada: Tomorrow's Giant, *1957*

Saskatchewan

The name Saskatchewan was given to the province by the Cree Indians. Knowing that the white man was on his way west, they figured on a plan to slow him down.

Ben Wicks, 1976

We can't understand why Alberta isn't more like Saskatchewan, home to the sunniest Canadians this side of Newfoundland. Saskatchewanians endure year after year of bad crops, bad weather and the Roughriders, yet remain resolutely, unreasonably optimistic. They are like Jimmy Hoffa's dog, sitting at the end of the driveway waiting for him to come home.

Jack Knox, Times Colonist,
January 16, 2005

"Doesn't it ever rain in Saskatchewan?" a tourist asked a native.

"Well let me put it to you this way," the native replied, "There are bullfrogs out on the edge of this town that are six years old and still don't know how to swim."

Robert Shelly, 1976

It was so dry in Saskatchewan during the Depression that the trees were chasing the dogs.

John Diefenbaker

Someone hastily erected his own road sign on Highway 9, on Saskatchewan soil, as he was entering Alberta in 1971:
THE LAST ONE OUT, TURN OUT THE LIGHT.

John Robert Colombo, 1983

Manitoba

Who has an I.Q. of 153?
153 Manitobans.

A former Manitoban

Alberta

"The image many people have of today's Alberta is one of two major cities surrounded by a whole bunch of cowboys and roughnecks, or rednecks, and horses and pickup trucks and pump jacks," Klein [Alberta's Premier] told Toronto's Empire Club of Canada. "There's much more to the province."

Times Colonist, *January 16, 2005*

Albirda:
Province at the western end of the prayer ease.
q.v. Noted for its natchual resources, among them gassa noil. There is a spool of Fie Narts at Bamf.

Mark M. Orkin in Canajan, eh?, *1973*

Sure there's more. Like shotguns, rye whiskey, big hats and small minds.

Jack Knox, Times Colonist, *January 16, 2005*

Quebec

Quebec is not a province like the others. More is a little more stupid.

Gerard Filion, 1962

For years Quebec has been the "sick man" of Canada; now that Quebec wants to stand on its own feet, suddenly everybody is complaining. It is as if the rich need to have the poor to look down upon.

Brian A. Brown, 1978

Ontario

In Toronto the Good, it's quite understood
That sin is a thing to beware-i-o!
But if you are bad, you've got to look sad,
For nothing is fun in Ontario.

Lister Sinclair, 1946

Premier Stanfield of Nova Scotia announces his Centennial project: To try to love Toronto.

The Toronto Star, *January 27, 1967*

British Columbia

Canadian guitar legend Kim Mitchell, in his fifties, joking about retirement:
 "I can picture myself in a few years out on the West Coast between Victoria and Nanaimo becoming a Birkenstock-wearing, backpacking, book reading, bicycling cedarhead and teaching little kids how to play guitar."

Times Colonist, *January 2, 2005*

Oh dear! Esquimalt is going to look silly again. A draft of the new Streets and Traffic Regulations No. 2607 surpasses even B.C.'s Safe Streets Acts by banning "squatting, kneeling, sitting or lying" on the sidewalk from 8 a.m. to 9 p.m., after which I presume we can all lawfully lie around in heaps. But if you drop to one knee to tie up your shoelaces before that, it's a $50 fine.

Alison Acker,
Esquimalt News, *February 9, 2005*

B.C., on the other hand, hangs around its bedroom in a ragged old Whistler UI Ski Team T-shirt, listening to Grateful Dead albums and muttering about maybe getting some work when they hold the 2010 Olympics. From Alberta's vantage point, B.C. is a lazy, granola-smoking, tree-hugging, commie wastrel. This clapped-out cliché is nonsensical, of course—sometimes we snort our granola.

Jack Knox, Times Colonist,
January 16, 2005

Nova Scotia

There is absolutely no truth to the rumour that the head of the fisherman's union in Nova Scotia is called "The Codfather."

Robert Shelley, 1976

Way Too Much Geography—Regions

IT IS NOT surprising that regional identities have developed in Canada. Stretching 6,500 kilometers across the continent, Canada is often thought of as a nation of regions, rather than a conglomerate of regions that make up a nation.

 The national football classic, the Grey Cup, pits the best of the East against the best of the West in a struggle which supposedly unites this country as no other single event can—yet the game divides about as much as it unites. You could argue for hockey being a prime factor in uniting this country. That's now all in the past—since we gave the sport over to the Americans to run.

Distinct regional identities are here to stay, despite government efforts over the past sixty years or so to relieve the resulting disparities through subsidizing development.

Regions (General)

Now we're not saying the West Coast of Canada is a haven for spaced-out, looney-tune, New Age, whacked-out flakes, but it is a fact that at any given moment 70% of the population of B.C. is chained to a tree. And the remaining 40% is attempting to cut it down. (I know the numbers don't add up but then, neither does B.C.)
Will Ferguson and Ian Ferguson,
How To Be A Canadian, *2007*

And that warning to outsiders:
What is black and blue and floats in the bay?
A mainlander after telling a Newfie joke.
William Kurelek, 1975

French Canada is a relic of the historical past preserved by isolation, as Siberian mammoths are preserved in ice.
Goldwin Smith,
Political Destiny of Canada, *1878*

It's always comforting to know that in any one election contest, only one of the candidates can be elected.
A wise old Maritimer

The way to defeat separatism is to recognize that Westerners and Maritimers have a similar complaint—that prosperity and power are centralized in Ontario.
Brian Brown, 1978

The Liberals have never had a leader from the Maritimes or from the West. Every Liberal Prime Minister has been from Central Canada. Perhaps this is one reason for their narrow vision on the national unity issue, not to mention economic problems and other matters from transportation to communication.

Brian A. Brown, 1978

Banner on C.P.R. express car in yard at Vancouver:
The First Carload of Kotex to Cross Canada.

Anon., 1927

We Westerners realize that even if there is snow on the roof that does not imply that the fire has gone out in the furnace.

John Diefenbaker, 1970

Dave Barrett recently called the Atlantic region "the economic looney bin of Canada."

Brian A. Brown, 1978

The North

On 1st of July, 1909, Captain Joseph-Elzéar Bernier claimed the Arctic Archipelago for Canada. Here's how he did it. "I took possession of Baffin Island for Canada in the presence of several Eskimos, and after firing nineteen shots I instructed an Eskimo to fire the twentieth, telling him he was now a Canadian."

John Robert Colombo, 1983

A missionary to Alberta stayed at an Indian village one evening. He asked the chief if it was safe to leave his belongings there. "Don't worry," the chief replied. "There isn't another white man around here for miles."

A Northerner

When I decided to bring before the people of Canada a plan for the development of the north, it was ridiculed. Liberal members, including Mr. Pearson the then leader of that Party, said we were going to build roads and railroads from igloo to igloo. Apparently he had been reading what was said in 1874 regarding Macdonald's plan to support the building of the C.P.R.: The Minister of Finance of that day suggested that Macdonald was endeavoring to build railroads from wigwam to wigwam.

John Diefenbaker, 1972

The far north, home of the Esk Moze, one of Canada's two founding races, *q.v.* of or pertaining to northern areas, Boreal.

The Ardic is one of the world's leading producers of snow benefitted for many years from a high world demand for this commodity which reached its peak during the gold rush of '98.

Mark M. Orkin in
Canajan, eh?, 1973

Referring to Diefenbaker's northern road program
From igloo to igloo.

Lester B. Pearson, 1958

In fact, our collective feeling for the North is pretty unimpressive. From Diefenbaker's Northern Vision through Arthur Laing's Operation Northland to that Arctic loss-leader Ookpik, all the whipped-up attempts to get us to Think North just haven't worked.

Graham Fraser, 1969

"Hell man," he shouted, "You can't leave the north. Once you're in it you can't get out." Why? His battered old face took on the deeper wrinkles of cerebration, and finally he explained everything. "It's the north," he said, "That's all. The north."

Bruce Hutchinson in Canada:
Tomorrow's Giant, *1957*

If I think now of the meals in North Bay, a cold shudder still comes over me. As to cleanliness, the less said the better. Nature is supposed to be kind by making one forget dark hours and keeping green the memory of happy ones. This does not apply to North Bay. I can never forget those meals.

The Possibilities of Canada
are Truly Great! Memoirs 1906–1924
by Martin Nordegg

We may not have gained much in ten years, but I think it's very possible that the government is opening the door back to an even earlier time when industry could do as it pleased. I can't see the situation improving for the environment in the North. It will likely get worse.

One thing has changed in ten years however. The R.C.M.P. are no longer holding seminars on native extremism and DIAND [Department of Indian and Northern Affairs] hired an R.C.M.P. official a few years ago as an enforcement advisor. The R.C.M.P. officer left the job a few months ago to go into Real Estate. He never saw one pollution case go to trial.

The Edmonton Journal,
January 6, 1985

"Pay no heed to [that guy]," the miner said. "He's nuts. Say, when I first hit this town she was the best damn town in the north. Thirty-five mines, ten thousand people, and whiskey two drinks for a quarter—and not watered down, like now. We was rich on a dollar and a half a day. That was 1917. Now she's dead. Two mines, two thousand people, and me too old to work."

Bruce Hutchinson in Canada:
Tomorrow's Giant, *1957*

The Yukon is a wonderful country for men and dogs but it kills women and horses.

Anon. old-timer, quoted in Amy V. Wilson's
No Man Stands Alone, *1969*

The tourist bureau for the Yukon Territory is trying to develop the northernmost part of that region into a honeymoon haven. After all, what honeymoon couple wouldn't go for a honeymoon night that was six months long?

Robert Shelly, 1976

Where are the Eskimo managers of Hudson's Bay Post? Where are the Eskimo police, the radio operators, the nurses? I'll tell you where they are. They're down at the welfare office drawing relief.

Duncan Pryde, Time, May 2, 1969

Well, it finally happened. A hotshot salesman actually succeeded in selling a refrigerator to an Eskimo. Six months later, the salesman returned to see how the family was doing with the appliance.

"It all right," the Eskimo told him. "But it take up too much time chopping ice to fit into little trays."

Robert Shelly, 1976

Apparently we have a third ocean no one ever noticed before because it was in the North, which always gets cropped out of the atlas to save space. Now, with global warming thinning the polar ice cap and getting the top of the page wet, many Canadians think we should embrace our Arctic, or at least give it a firm handshake.

Jack Knox, March 12, 2006

The North gets so cold that the words you speak freeze the second they leave your mouth. Someone has to thaw them out in a frying pan to know what you said.

A Northerner

East Vs. West

Regional stereotypes exist even in business. The dark-suited tycoons of Toronto contrast sharply with "cool" western executives.

Jeanette Harris, 1976

A leading pollster once described psychographics for me like this: "In most of Canada, a man of 60 is 60. On the West Coast the 60-year-old man thinks he is 40, the 40-year-old man thinks he's 25 and the 25-year-old man thinks he's always going to be 25." In short, pure demos fly out of the window. We're all out there, kayaking and jogging and snowboarding and pretending we're forever younger than we really are.

Ian Haysom, 2003

Easterners are so snobbish and Westerners are so anti-snobbish that we are sometimes snobbish about that.

High School student from Moose Jaw on a CBC Special called Seeing for Ourselves?

From the same decade [1950s] comes the following, from a Nova Scotian privy:
WHY GO WEST WHEN YOU CAN MAKE YOUR PILE HERE?

John Robert Colombo, 1975

Some Easterners seem to think that they can just go out West, stand up in Calgary, call the Prime Minister of Canada a horse's behind, and think they're going to unite the country. They are forgetting that the people out west love horses!

Dave Broadfoot, 1974

"You know," I said, "I'd like to live in Toronto, it's such a lovely city. But to really understand what is happening in Canada it is necessary to live where the action is, such as Quebec or the West."

Brian A. Brown, 1978

Once I picked up a hitchhiker out West and when I told him I was from the East he got right out of the car.

Harold Fishleigh, November 25, 1955

CANADIANS: SERIOUSLY HUMOROUS

The People—Who We Are

WE HAVE LOOKED at the vast differences in the Canadian environment and how the factors of climate, distance, geography, and landscape have affected the people since they first arrived at this landmass that we now call Canada. Those environmental factors, plus the many countries from which immigrants have come from over the past 400 years, have helped to produce Canada's extreme diversities in culture, outlook, and social experience; in fact, in every area of society. I would be remiss in not mentioning our neighbours to the south, the Americans, and the influence they have had on the development of that diversity. Soon after Confederation, Canadians exhibited a kind of split personality in dual loyalties that remains to this day. We were North Americans, but did not want to abandon or modify in any way our European heritage. We also did not want to be gobbled up by the United States. Therefore, the continued ties with our European heritage helped to balance the overwhelming influence of our great neighbour to the south.

The first settlers came to Canada, some reluctantly, for many different reasons; some to escape religious persecution, to find new freedoms, some to escape political persecution, and some just to seek out new opportunities that did not exist in their previous homelands. The first settlers were predominately English and French and, up to perhaps the end of the Second World War, that pattern of English and French continued. Since then, what has been added is a very cosmopolitan mix of immigrants—which has had a tremendous impact on virtually every area of the heritage of those people who had previously settled this land.

Canada has always been tremendously influenced by forces outside its own boundaries, and Canadians do not identify themselves just as Canadians, for we are a nation of joiners. We are firstly Maritimers, Newfoundlanders, Quebecers, Westerners or some other such designation. The part appears to be more important than the whole. We join churches, amateur sports clubs, parent-teacher associations, veterans clubs and any other organizations that make us feel as though we belong somewhere. Unfortunately, the commonalities which join Canadians also help to separate us.

The People (General)

Explanation to a police officer who stopped him for speeding:
I wasn't driving too fast, I was flying too low.

Philip A. Gaglardi, 1975

I went to the Kremlin to see that big dill pickle they keep there, whatshisname, Lenin. I left a Maple Leaf sticker on the railing at his tomb. I also [relieved myself] in Red Square.

Harold Ballard
in The Advocate, *January 9, 1985*

There's only one me, and I'm stuck with him.

Robert L. Stanfield, 1973

You damned pup, I'll slap your chops for you!

Sir John A. Macdonald to Sir Oliver Mowat,
House of Assembly, April 19, 1861

"I guess you heard about Mayor Drapeau's accident?"
"No, what happened?"
"He was out taking his usual morning walk—and a motorboat hit him."

Robert Shelly, 1976

I owe a lot to my teachers and mean to pay them back some day.

Steven Leacock, "The children's corner"
in College Days, *1923*

To be Prime Minister of Canada, you need the hide of a rhinoceros, the morals of St. Francis, the patience of Job, the Wisdom of Solomon, the strength of Hercules, the leadership of Napoleon, the magnetism of a Beatle and a subtlety of Machiavelli.

Lester B. Pearson, 1964

I could not have called him [John G. Diefenbaker] a S.O.B. I did not know he was one at that time.

John F. Kennedy, 1961

R.B. Bennett was a tough guy; he wants to be kissed.
Robert Edwards, 1973

People don't expect us to keep election promises.
*Harvie Andrie, speaking on the CBC
just after his election in September 1984,*
The Calgary Sun, *January 3, 1985*

A British Columbian is a man who has a California-style house, a Montreal mortgage, an English car, and a Scottish dog. His wife, who comes from Regina or maybe it is Calgary, either has a cat whose forbears came from Persia or a small bird from the tropics which she keeps in a cage allegedly imported from eastern Canada, but more likely made in Japan.
Barry Mather, in John Robert Colombo's
101 Canadian Place Names, *1983*

These Canadians are an ambivalent lot—one minute they want to be peacekeepers, next minute they punch the hell out of each other on the ice rink.
Ken Wiwa,
The Globe and Mail, *July 1, 2003*

Everything I did, I wish I had done better. I wasn't big enough, smart enough to do better.
Joseph R. Smallwood, 1972

Pierre Elliott Trudeau, carried to the nations highest office in 1968 on a wave of adulation, departed in 1984 on a riptide of criticism. John Turner, the supposed inheritor of the magus mantle, bravely marched his Liberal army up the hill on September 4, 1984, and was badly wounded by the charges of patronage. When he looked back to see how his troops were doing, he found them lying down, hiding or sliding off to enemy camps.
The Financial Post, *December 29, 1984*

With such a nose and face you dare not look
In the still lake or in the tranquil brook;
Or else you're sure to meet Narcissus' fate—
He died from love of self, you'll die of hate.
>> Upper Canada Almanac, *1837*

Jones observed an old lady sitting across the room.
"For heaven's sake!" he remarked to Robinson, "Who is that extraordinarily ugly woman there?"
"That," answered Robinson, "is my wife."
Jones was taken aback, but moved up front again.
"Well," he said persuasively, "You ought to see mine!"
>> *Bob Edwards,*
>> from A Treasury of Canadian Humour
>> by Robert Thomas Allan, *1967*

Ah, John A., John A., how I love you! How I wish I could trust you!
>> *Anon., 1863, on Sir John A. Macdonald*

People from every corner of the world are coming to Canada, on arrival, looking around to see that they are surrounded by people from the other three corners.
>> *Pico Lyer, "The Last Refuge,"*
>> Harper's, *June, 2002*

Brian Mulroney, speaking on television in Saskatoon before the election: "The day after a Conservative government is sworn in there'll be tens of thousands of new jobs."
Brian Mulroney, speaking on television in Ottawa after the election: "I never said any such thing."
>> The Calgary Sun,
>> *January 3, 1985*

I don't want to sound presumptuous, but Mackenzie King was dull, too.
>> *Robert L. Stanfield, 1967*

My test of a true Canadian is to ask him if he is an American. The reaction is nearly as bad as calling a Kiwi an Aussie.

orangespeeddemon, 1998

When I first arrived I dated several Canadian males, only to find that we were incompatible. On the first date they would take me to dinner and in return, invariably expect Everything.

...So now I date men from Australia, England, India and the Philippines—my only rule is: No Canadians. I like them as conversationalists, they're welcomed guests at parties in our apartment but that's all. On a date, they frankly scare me.

Young female immigrant, 1971

A young man, an only son, married against his parents wishes. Afterward, in telling a friend how to break the news to them, he said: "Start off by telling them that I'm dead, and then gently work up to the climax."

Bob Edwards from A Treasury of Canadian Humour *by Robert Thomas Allan, 1967*

One of the peculiarities of becoming a celebrity in Canada, however minor, is that people are constantly coming up to remind you who you are.

Peter C. Newman,
Here Be Dragons: Telling Tales of People, Passion, and Power, *2004*

Women

So far as my observation goes, nobody's wife or sisters or daughters want to take a hand in politics, but all the noise comes from those unattached women who, having dismally failed as females, turned desperate and covetous eyes upon having male prerogatives.

Saturday Night, May 1893

If women keep on demanding a vote, cropping their hair, opposing us in the professions, wearing our coats, hats and shirts, and if men continue nursing babies, promoting female dress reform, and using curling tongs, first thing we know there will be a blurred line denoting a merging of the sexes. That would be a fine development in human anatomy with which to mark the close of the nineteenth century.

Saturday Night, *May, 1893*

All are grossly overweight and spend their every waking hour flogging themselves with exercises in the frantic effort to get into a size 10 dress. Once into her size 10 she decides all is not as it should be. Her top is too small. The cure? A bra that crosses the heart. Her rear sticks out. The answer? Tight panty hose to pull it in. She is now the shape of an ice-cream cone. A true Canadian beauty.

Ben Wicks, 1976

Behind every great man there's a woman rolling her eyes.

Jim Carey

Again, what history book records the name of that decisive Canadian (probably a woman) who sat down one day and, in a prodigious act of imagination, combined buffalo meat with blueberries, added grease, and produced pemmican on the Canadian prairie? Nobody knows that woman, though she had discovered the compliment of the canoe...

Meanwhile, the Mountie had his binoculars trained upon her and was giving the lady a careful and thorough-going study.

At last, he came to the decision that she wouldn't do. He dispatched his orderly with a note of regret and sufficient funds to send the woman back to her home.

"Laughter in the West,"
Old Days and Old Timers, *date unknown*

Women have proved to be more honest, courageous, and hardworking, but this is no reason not to have more of them in government.

Eric Nicol,
Canadian Politics Unplugged, *2003*

In 1972, the suspicion that Canadian females are superior to males was confirmed by a scientific study! Canadian women no longer can be called the weaker sex. Pound for pound Canadian women are stronger than Canadian men up to the age of 40. In almost every age group women score more than 20% higher than men in a key fitness measurement called V02, which is the ability to take in and utilize oxygen during effort...

Bob Pennington, 1972

The Canadian girl shows a decided aptitude for commanding; there is none of the Anglo-Saxon belief that woman is the weaker vessel. Woman's rights movements makes small progress in Canada, because the Canadian woman gets what she wants without let or hindrance: because she has so many privileges, the right to vote on a subject in which she takes little or no interest seems not worth striving for. Canadian legislators are quicker to grant privileges to women than Canadian women are to demand them. The average girl possesses an impulsive force or magnetism that makes its conquests without strife.

Hector Charlesworth, 1893

Events in the legislature suggest the well-known toast, "Here is to woman, once our superior, now our equal."

Eyeopener, *March 18, 1916*

They make it all. The women were the ones that made the good times. The men, all they did was sit around and yack.

Mrs. Inez Hendersen of Hythe, Alberta
Interview, 1974

On occasion somebody called out to Nellie McClung, "Where are your children, while you're out speaking?" She said, "My children are at home with their father—the only 'parent' the law allows." At that time mothers had no right to the children at all. A father could will away his child to somebody else!

Mrs. Rodger, Past President,
Alberta Women's Institute, Interview, 1924

As a coddled Canadian who spent a couple of winters in England, I descend into the basement at the beginning of every autumn and kiss the furnace full on the damper. I do this because a series of flats and houses in London taught me that women are wonderful, money is more so, but there is really nothing like central heating.

Eric Nicol, from
Shall We Join The Ladies?, 1972

We have seen thee, Queen of Cheese,
Lying quietly at your ease,
Gently fanned by evening breeze
Thy fair form no flies dare sees.

James McIntyre, late 1800s

"Why should women worry about possessing some of their husband's property during his lifetime?" he asked. "Time enough after he's dead!"

Hon. Charles W. Cross, former
Attorney-General of Alberta, 1976

Canada is a woman's paradise. It is nothing of the kind. A woman's life in Canada is extremely hard, and lonely, and it is because of their loneliness that the asylums...They're being filled with women, who are driven mad by their loneliness. They are caged in a "shack" often miles from any populated district. Turn your back on Canada."

Moose Jaw Evening Times, *June 28, 1913*

To be let, or to be sold, for the term of her life
Elizabeth Hall—by the way of a wife:
She's old and she's ugly, ill-natured and thin
For further particulars inquire within.

Upper Canada Almanac, 1837

In the biblical account, God first created Adam and then, from his rib, formed the first woman. The preeminence of the male in western society may be traced to this creation story. Had the bible been written in Canada, one suspects that order of creation might have been reversed, for in our society the female appears to have an innate superiority over the male.

The Canadian woman has long been the object of veneration, respect and fear, and her praises have been sung since the earliest days of our history. The charms of French-Canadian girls in particular have received glowing tributes as seen in this account written in 1844.

Raymond Reid in The Canadian Style, *1973*

You did everything by hand, everything the hard way, and I think the women...did just as much to make this western country as any of the men did. They were just taken for granted—that was their job, they were supposed to do that. Men, of course, they got blowed up about what they did. They were supposed to do theirs too, but they got talked about where the women didn't. Women sat in the background while the men got praised.

Mrs. Inez Hendersen, Hythe, Alta., Interview, 1974

I never realized until my first campaign in 1921 what miserable incompetent creatures women were in the eyes of the public. I ought to have developed a terrible inferiority complex by the time it was over, for practically the only issue that seemed to concern the electorate or the opposition, was that I was a woman and worse an Englishwoman.

Irene Parlby, What Business Have Women in Politics?, *Circa 1935*

On doing home repairs and improvements:
How hard can it be?

> Mag Ruffman, "ToolGirl," on
> Anything I Can Do

Men

There was once a young man from Saint John's
Whose preference in girls was for blondes.
    But yet if he met
    a brunette who would pet,
He would date her without any qualms.

> John Robert Colombo, 1975

Baie-Comeau barber, Emile Germain, remembers Brian Mulroney's head, particularly its cowlick:
"He was a difficult haircut."

> The Globe and Mail,
> December 7, 1984

Canadian males seem afraid of women. At cocktail parties guests soon isolate into groups of one sex; at dances the women are granted territorial rights to one side of the hall. Until reaching Canada I had never heard of the custom 'boys night out', which still seems a disgusting sort of habit. For example, the men in my office were always puzzled when I declined to join them for lunch. Of course I wasn't interested. I preferred a young woman as my lunch time companion.

> Bob Pennington, 1972

Old men who pull up their trousers to their nipples: "Where do you get zippers that long?"

> Anon., 1905

In general, men don't like to think about the subject of castration. Canadian men really don't like to going to see a dentist because of a deep-seated fear of castration.

Psychologist Brad Rempel, 2005

What Canadian men like to do when he is drunk is to have sex. It seldom happens though.

John Flattery, 1999

Farmers

Do you know that in Central Canada they think "combines" are some kind of restrictive business deals? I was happy to learn that anti-combines legislation was not another measure against farmers. In the West we need all the good combines we can get.

Brian A. Brown, 1978

Stubble-jumper:
 slang: a prairie farmer.

Katherine Barber,
Only in Canada, You Say, 2007

Ten years ago the deficit on my farm was about a hundred dollars; but by well designed capital expenditure, by drainage and by greater attention to details, I have got it into the thousands.

Steven Leacock, in his preface to
Sunshine Sketches, *1912*

In Canada, there was a drought last year and everyone talked in terms of the amount of money lost. In Mozambique, when there is drought, you talk of the number of lives lost.

CUSO worker Yvon Madore, in
The Globe and Mail, *December 15, 1984*

Getting Around & Communicating

CANADIAN DEVELOPMENT AND survival has depended on transportation and communication ever since the first European explorers set foot on North American soil. For years, shipments of vital supplies from Europe kept the fledgling Canadian settlements from extinction. Railways expanded that vital service as they established links to more settled regions. Over the years, railways—as people movers—have diminished in importance, but the use of railways to move goods has increased.

Transportation and communication were inextricably intertwined and dependent on each other. The need in Canada to bridge the immense distances between regions and settlements has made Canada a leader in the world of communications. Such a bridge could not have been built without public and private enterprise working together. It is a special relationship that continues today in dominating the economic lives of Canadians.

In travelling from the past to the present, we also see the impact of the automobile and the exploits of aircraft in opening up this country. The five modes of transportation are water, rail, motor carrier, air and pipeline. There is an intense competition between most of those modes of transportation as each provides transport alternatives for people and goods.

The e-commerce revolution—indeed, the immediate nature of e-commerce—is prodding the transportation industry to deliver people and goods, not only more cheaply, but more efficiently than ever before.

The importance of transportation and communication to a trading nation such as Canada cannot be underestimated. These systems must remain highly efficient in order to compete on the world stage.

The Railway

The Canadian Pacific Railway was given a bit of a line here and a bit of a line there and almost as much land as it wanted, and the laughter was still going on when the last spike was driven between east and west.

Rudyard Kipling, 1920

The Canadian railroad system is largely the creation of American money.

Samuel E. Moffett, 1972

When the CP railroad was expanding its lines, it ran into some strong opposition from a farmer who refused to let the company run track across his land...despite the fact that the railroad offered him twenty times what the land was worth.

"But why in the world are you turning down such a generous offer?" the railway agent asked.

"Because," the farmer replied, "I'll be damned if I'm going to keep running out to the barn day and night to open and shut the door every time you fellows want to run the train through!"

Robert Shelly, 1976

The Grand Trunk Railway governs Canada at the present moment. Its power is paramount. The Ministry are mere puppets in its hands and dance whatever tune the Company pipes.

Toronto Globe, *April 22, 1857*

We seem to forget that a healthy snort or two is part of this country's tradition. Without it, we would never have built Niagara Falls. And without those early railroad men on the bottle, today we wouldn't be able to enjoy that wonderful winding trip through the Rockies. It would have been straight.

*Roger Abbott, Don Ferguson
and John Morgan in*
The AirFarce Book, *1980*

From a Canadian Transport Commission report circa 1960, which says the Crown Corporation's 30-year-old equipment is "on the verge of collapse," and asks: "Is no one in charge?"

"No other railway in the industrialized world entrusts its mainline services to a fleet of locomotives as old, outdated and obsolete as does VIA; no other railway could afford to do so.

"What we have here is a story of decades of neglect, decline and indecision, followed by only a short period of rebuilding."

*VIA President Pierre Franche,
who admits VIA is operating
"museum pieces," circa 1990*

The Media

People won't accept my style of news. I use slang, cuss words, sex. Some of my acquaintances are garbage men, harlots, newsboys, waitresses. I get drunk. I exaggerate. I don't believe in goodness.
                                                  Gordon Sinclair, 1944

I now quote from a newspaper that worships at the altar of Liberalism. I refer to the *Winnipeg Free Press*.
                                                  John Diefenbaker, 1967

Canadian Broadcasting Corporation:
The CBC has never learned how to let an individual make a career of his own talent.
                                        Andrew Allan, The Globe and Mail,
                                                  January 16, 1971

Why the CBC must be dull:
When the Government owns a medium of expression, that medium becomes consciously an instrument of power. To disguise power one must be dull. Dullness is the only form which makes power acceptable or tolerable— a fact which accounts for the solemn masks worn by top executives and their imitators.
                                            Marshall McLuhan, February 1957

Headline:
ANOTHER BLOW FOR UNLUCKY FAMILY
Ted Kennedy survives crash.
                                        The Ottawa Journal, *June 20, 1964*

I think cartoons serve a very useful purpose. I see all the cartoons. Macdonald used to say he had the ugliest face of anyone of his time, but if Macdonald could see the cartoons today, he would conclude that he's in second place. As for the critics, wow, big-game hunters don't go after gophers!
                                                  John Diefenbaker, 1967

From the infancy of the nation Canada has had an able and vigorous newspaper press. It has been tensely Canadian in sentiment, but in everything else it has been American.

Mr. Goldwin Smith, 1922

Not since ancient time has a war been fought of which the people at home knew so little while it was in progress. There are no war correspondents. Only officials, appointed to tell the public what they are willing to tell the enemy, are permitted to send us any news.

Saturday Night,
October, 1915

CANADIANS: SERIOUSLY HUMOROUS

Politics and Government

CANADIANS FIND FAULT in a never-ending way about the quality of political life and behaviour throughout every region of this country. They express an intense disdain of the politicians themselves, both federal and provincial, but are unwilling to bring their complaints to a fruitful end by engaging themselves in an intelligent manner in the political life of their country.

Once in a while an honest straightforward specimen of a politician is elected to office. Soon however, the people, perchance for hearing what they want to hear and the absurdities of the party he represents, soon steer him into a political mainstream that dictates that the main objective is to get reelected. Canadians don't want to hear the truth from their politicians, and if those politicians dare to defy convention, then they are driven from office at the next ballot—if, in fact, they even survive the first ballot.

Politics (General)

Parliament Buildings:
Those buildings in Ottawa will be admirably suited for lunatic asylums, whenever the town is sufficiently prosperous to require them for that purpose.

N. A. Woods, 1860

Former Postmaster-General André Ouellet, introducing a series of postage stamps featuring the portraits of past Prime Ministers of Canada:
If a letter is late, we can always look at the stamp and say, well that figures, he was a master of delay.

André Ouellet, 1976

In an increasingly complacent and a conservative society, there is a great risk of speaking out about any social, political, or moral issue for fear of offending one's senior, crusty old colleagues.

Jack MacLeod, Professor,
University of Toronto, 1984

Canada's history is as dull as ditchwater, and her politics is full of it.

Maurice Hutton, 1935

Politicians and Political Parties

Being leader of the Canadian Alliance must be like playing Whack-A-Mole. You stand there, coiled tight as a spring, mallet in hand, just waiting for one of your guys to pop up and say something goofy. Then—whammo!—you smack him on the head, driving him back into his hole. This is known as hammering out party policy.

Jack Knox,
Times Colonist, *2003*

A sticker on the window of a car parked at a Progressive Conservative campaign rally:
Politicians are like diapers;
they need to be changed often, and for the same reason.

The Globe and Mail,
September 29, 2003

Mobster? Dealer?
Sure. But...hey...I'm no Liberal!

Krieger's View,
The Province, *2003*

Columnist Don Martin commenting on the election of low-key Stephane Dion as Liberal leader and soft-spoken Ed Stelmach as leader of the Alberta Tories:
"There's a new Canadian formula to winning a party leadership: Start third; stay bland; let the two titans knock each other out; listen for the sound of jaws hitting the floor at the moment of victory."

The Province,
December 5, 2006

It is a shame that leaders of Canada's two right-wing parties cannot manage to put all their egos in one basket.

Dave Duncan, Calgary,
The Globe and Mail, *September 29, 2003*

Voting for clarification:
Paul Martin:
A vote for the Bloc Quebecois is a vote for Stephen Harper.
Jack Layton:
A vote for the Green Party is a vote for Paul Martin.
Ujjal Dosanjh:
A vote for the NDP is a vote for the Conservatives.
Okay, I want to vote for the Green Party.
Could someone tell me who to vote for?

Norman Abbey, Nanaimo,
Times Colonist, *September, 2004*

Patronage

I don't know what is marijuana. Perhaps I will try it when it will no longer be criminal. I will have my money for my fine and a joint in the other hand.

Prime Minister Jean Chretien
The Province, *October 5, 2003*

Prime Minister Jean Chretien says he may decide to try marijuana after he retires and it is decriminalized. Well, he had me fooled. Based on his behaviour, I thought he had been stoned for years.

Doug Charles, Langley,
The Province, *October 26, 2003*

Congratulations Ontario. By putting Stephen Harper in charge of the Conservative party, you've just guaranteed that moderation is a swear word, that rednecks in pickup trucks will overrun Toronto and that if Conservatives win the next election, the Queen's visage on the loonie will be replaced by a cowboy hat to commemorate Alberta's entry into Confederation in 1905. Yee haw.

Mark Milke, 2004

We farmers first will work on the principle that the hog be the one to be killed off first.

> John Oliver, Premier of British Columbia,
> about 1920, on patronage

Politicians

Your scandalous behaviour disqualifies you from running for the NDP. Why not give the Liberals a call?

> National Post, *April 16, 2004*

Like actors and priests, politicians are professional spellbinders, experts in the art of mumbo-jumbo. I defy anyone to translate the meaning of anything [which] that most able and honourable politician, Premier William Davis, has said in public throughout his long term.

> *McKenzie Porter, 1985*

Canadian prime ministers are responsible for some great lines. [At the time Otto Lang was the Minister responsible for the Canadian Wheat Board.]

[An] Easterner asked what M.F. on all that farm equipment was. His host, the Rt. Hon. John Diefenbaker, replied that it meant Master Farmer.

"Then what about POOL on all those tall buildings. They are not pools obviously."

"I don't like to tell you what the P is for," said Mr. Diefenbaker, "but the rest stands for On Otto Land."

> *Brian A. Brown, 1978*

The people of Canada get better government than they deserve.

> *Sir John Willison, 1919*

Mr. Howe determines what is to be done. Mr. St. Laurent agrees. The rest of the cabinet says, "me too," and the one hundred eighty-seven other Liberals add "amen."

John Diefenbaker, 1957

Mitchell Hepburn (at an Ontario political meeting where a manure spreader was used as a platform):
"This is the first time I've ever been on a Tory platform."
Tory voice:
"Throw her into high, Mitch, she's got the biggest load now she'll ever have."

*Library of Parliament
for the sundry excerpts
from* Throop's Scrap Book,
by Hector Charlesworth

Cabinet:
Give me better wood and I will make you a better cabinet.

*Sir John A. Macdonald,
a reply sometimes made to criticisms
of his choice of cabinet ministers*

House of Commons

There is a place in Canada where nobody is out of work.

The minimum wage has just been raised to $72,500 a year. Nobody is poor or powerless or without influence. Everyone enjoys privileges, including the right to make speeches on television.

The place is the House of Commons, with 282 members supposedly representing the people of Canada.

*Don McGillivary,
Calgary Herald,
January 2, 1985*

In theory the Commons can do anything; in practice; it can do little.

John N. Turner, 1968

Lawyers who represent 0.07% of the population as a whole account for 22.64% of the members of the House of Commons. Housewives who represent approximately 31% of the population of the whole are represented in the Federal Cabinet by one person or .0037%. Carpenters who, believe it or not, represent almost one half of one percent of the population are not represented in the House of Commons. Teachers comprise 1.61% of the population and .064% of the House of Commons.

How about women aside from occupations. Women must represent about one half of the population and yet the number of women in the House of Commons is only 2.14%.

Julian Smith,
Rules to Keep the Rascals Out, *1978*

Senate

An absurdly effete body.

Lord Dufferin, 1874

We have one, mind you only one, really well-run home for the aged and infirmed (prematurely or otherwise) and it is called the Senate.

Harold Town, 1964

Edward Blake was reduced to protesting, "Mr. Speaker, the country is led by a drunkard."

"Yes, Mr. Speaker," retorted Macdonald, "I am drunk, but the Honourable Member is a fool and tomorrow I will be sober…"

Brian Brown, 1978

Intellectuals

A reporter asked me following the 1979 election: "Well, Jack, aren't you happy having a Westerner as Prime Minister?" I have never known my reaction to be stronger. It just welled up: "Clark, a Westerner? For heaven's sake he can't even ride a horse!"

Jack Horner, in
My Own Brand

Intellectuals in large numbers will sink the raft of any party, and if allowed to write a program will kill it.

Harold A. Innis, 1935

"I'll appoint Grits and New Democrats to political jobs," went Mulroney's favourite line. "But not until there isn't a single breathing Tory left to take one."

The Financial Post,
December 29, 1984

...bunch of Liberal rejects.

Brian Mulroney on the Senate, 1985

I have no politics, I am a Canadian.

George McCullagh, 1966

Federal Budget

You can never spend more than you have, otherwise you have endless inflation.

Pierre Trudeau, Mclean's,
October 20, 1975

This budget is intended to show that we really mean business in the fight against inflation.
Finance Minster Edgar Benson,
Budget Speech, June 1969

This budget reflects my determination to deal with inflation...it recognizes the need to all government including this one responsible to parliament to restrain spending."
Finance Minister John Turner,
Budget Speech, May 6, 1974

Our goals are clear; our first objective must be to maintain the underlying trend to lower inflation.
Finance Minister Donald McDonald,
Budget Speech, March 1977

We expect by year end that inflation will be down at 6%.
Finance Minister Jean Cretien,
January 20, 1978

H.R.H. Charles, Prince of Wales, to Joe Clark about the confidence vote, which Clark had rejected, regarding his leadership:
What I don't understand is, why was 67% not enough?
Governor General's Dinner,
Ottawa, June 20, 1983

New Democratic Party

Claims of membership sign-up abuse prompts closer look at Federal Liberal antics:
"We're so proud of Bootsie...seems that she helped put Paul Martin into the Prime Minister's Office."
Victoria News, *2004*

I'd rather waffle to the left than waffle to the right.

Ed Broadbent, 1969

Liberals

The metric system:
...they brought in metric so no one can understand what's going on...the Liberal theme song is 'Nothing could be sweeter than to fool you with the litre'.

Patrick Martin, Ellen Gregg, George Perlin in
Contenders, The Tory Quest for Power, *1983*

William Lyon Mackenzie King:
Mackenzie King was the antithesis of John A.—a Liberal rather than a Conservative, short rather than tall, given to fat rather than sinew, tidy straight hair instead of an unruly thatch, and absolutely no charisma. While John A. loved to wear tartan jackets and red ties, Mackenzie King preferred suitable suits. To put it bluntly, he was rather a dull old stick.

Carlotta Hacker, 1981

For the first time since 1867, we don't have a single Liberal government in Canada.

Judd Buchanan in The Financial Post,
December 29, 1984

Allan MacEachen's "reform" budget of November, 1981, was so bad, Crosbie told them, that he was forced to "throw off this reform and then that one," [Crosbie pretended to cast off his garments] "until he was left naked as a newt. He became the Gypsy Rose Lee of Canadian politics!"

Patrick Martin, Ellen Gregg, George Perlin in
Contenders, The Tory Quest for Power, *1983*

Canadair...it should be called How Can They Dare!

> Patrick Martin, Ellen Gregg, George Perlin in
> Contenders, The Tory Quest for Power, 1983

Conservatives

An English tourist in Canada was being shown the sites of Ottawa by a professional guide. The Englishman finally asked, "Who is that old man walking round and round Parliament House muttering to himself?"

The guide replied after a glance, "Oh! That is Mr. Bennett, sir, Prime Minister of the Dominion. He is holding a meeting of the Cabinet."

> Library of Parliament
> for the sundry excerpts
> from Throop's Scrap Book
> by Hector Charlesworth

There are more votes on Main Street than Bay Street.

> John Diefenbaker in Peter Newman's
> Renegade in Power

C.C.F. friends over there are all full of an abundance of hot air and heifer dust.

> Hon W. R. Motherwell,
> House of Commons, 1934

The Conservatives have been searching for another Sir John A. Macdonald, and when a new leader turned out to be an ordinary mortal he was subjected to constant criticism until he was forced to resign.

> John R. Williams, 1956

They said I was anti-Quebec, and I said to them, "Produce one line, one word that shows I was ever against Quebec." They couldn't do it.

John Diefenbaker, 1964

Rural constituents like to know their member firsthand by name, to be able to stop him on the street and talk to him. In the cities this degree of familiarity is never achieved. Clark would have been able to breeze into Calgary and it wouldn't really have mattered which part of Calgary he was in; the media would make the entire city his constituency. This argument didn't carry any weight with Clark either. He was determined to be "the boy from High River!" And this was the man who once admitted he was so fearful of horses that not even as a school kid would he pat one on the nose!

*Jack Horner,
in* My Own Brand

"I remember 10 years ago, you coming up our way campaigning," she said, "we called you 'Snowy Joe' 'cause you always seemed to bring the snow when you came." Snowy Joe looked about ready for the mountains as he smiled and tried to move away. "You've come along way," she concluded. "At lease they don't call you 'Joe Who' anymore."

Mrs. Edna Campbell, 1983

When Little Jack Horner came back to Edmonton recently with a gift from the pork barrel, one and a half million dollars for the Commonwealth Games facilities, he tried to present it at half-time in a football game. As soon as he was introduced the booing became so great that he was drowned right out. The pork barrel doesn't work, changing parties doesn't work, nothing really works.

Brian Brown, 1978

Satan saw my picture in *Newsweek*, and said he never knew he had such opposition in Canada.

John Diefenbaker, 1963

In Quebec the Conservative Party is a pretty lively corpse.
*J.G.H. Bergeron, speech in Toronto,
December 14, 1905*

Well, Sir Wilfrid, I can't waste any more time; I have to sell my papers.
*John Diefenbaker,
as a young newsboy,
talking to Sir Wilfrid Laurier*

Civil Servants

Civil servants in the Federal Transport Department are being taught how to ride in elevators and on escalators. The instructions are in a twenty-four page booklet issued by the Department to encourage its employees to treat their offices as "a home away from home." On using washrooms—"refrain from depositing foreign objects in toilets, urinals and sinks—all washrooms are equipped with receptacles for this purpose."
*Vancouver Sun,
February 2, 1977*

Overheard on the street:
"They say," one business man was commenting to another, "that if the postal unions get what they're asking for, the cost of postage will go up to thirty cents a stamp."
"I've got news for you. It already costs a dollar eight to mail a letter in Canada."
"What do you mean?"
"Eight cents for the stamp and a dollar for the telephone call to see if it got there."
Two businessmen, 1976

Civil Servant Quiz:
Most civil servants with part-time jobs moonlight as:
   A. Display-window mannequins
   B. Mattress testers
   C. Gravestones.

*Roger Abbott, Don Ferguson, John Morgan
in* The Air Farce Book, *1980*

You may wonder why I'm writing in red ink. Thought it was for Christmas didn't you and I bet you said, "How Gauche!"
Well it happens to be a government-issue accounting pen and they only come in red. This is appropriate as my department hasn't been in the black for years.

Mary M. Oman and Darell Robinson,
Canadian Pornography,
Book Two, *1981*

If you have played chess, you will easily recognize the pawns that's us, the voters, no choice but to plod onward. Then there are the rooks—they represent the civil service moving in straight lines up and down the board looking neither left or right. They have their job to do and reduplication does not bother them. Nor are they required to do anything creative.

Brian A. Brown, 1978

RCMP

The RCMP, which had always been in the spy game with its Security and Intelligence Directorate, had a field day throughout the '50s and early '60s, trampling on the rights of privacy, free speech, free association, and even the right to have the wrong relatives.

Walter Stewart, 1976, But Not in Canada

Mountie: Canadian icon, strong of jaw, red of coat, pure of heart, busy with government fraud.

Graham Hicks, 2004

Arsey Em Pee:
A paramilitary police body combining features of the army (red coats), the civil service (red tape), the secret service (Red hunting), and politics (red herrings). Also known as "The Mounties."

Mark M. Orkin in Canajan, eh?, *1973*

...and the hassling of the family of a fifteen-year-old Winnipeg boy who wrote a letter to the paper suggesting that Santa Claus must be a commie, because he wore a red suit and gave away presents, which was bound to undermine the free enterprise system. The boy's parents were warned—I'm not making this up, it happened in 1964—to curb his dangerous beliefs.

Walter Stewart, 1976

Armed Forces

"What! I modernize the Navy and abandon to blazes five hundred years of tradition!"

Norris, The Vancouver Sun, *from a cartoon*

There's room for you in Canada's armed forces too! Get to go on cane nable manoeuvres in a genuine boat. (subject to availability of boat.) Thrill to challenging NATO exercises: While American war ships fire armour-piercing shells, you'll proudly stand behind safe, unloaded guns and shout "Bang." It's peaceful, it's Canadian, and it's effective. The enemy will die laughing.

The Air Farce Book *by Roger Abbott, Don Ferguson, John Morgan, 1980*

Privatizing our national security:
Aircraft shortage is just the latest example of how our once-strong military has lost its way. It's as if the police were to rely on taxi-drivers to watch out for crime.

> Times Colonist,
> *September 27, 2003*

Laurier's Tin-Pot Navy:
Term used by opponents to Laurier's navy policy.

> *1909, and later*

We are Canadians here and we don't want any peregrinating Imperialists to dictate our defense policies...We in Canada can take care of our policies, defense and others.

> *Ian Mackenzie, Minister of National Defense,*
> *in answer to a statement by Viscount Elibank,*
> *Toronto, August 19, 1936*

A piece of aircraft navigational equipment which costs $9,000, and had a replacement value of $15,000, was sent to be repaired at an R.C.A.F. base. By error it was declared surplus and sold for $20.

> *Auditor General, 1977*

The Royal Canadian Air Force now is [a] handmaiden of the U.S. Strategic Air Force and nothing more...a colonial military instrument serving the nuclear strategy of the U.S.

> *Major General Macklin, 1958*

Them and Us

MANY CANADIANS BELIEVE they live in a classless society; if they do, they are burying their heads in the sand of a middle and lower class delusion.

A perennial "them and us" conflict pervades our society which, at times, results in open hostility. Country folks versus the city slickers, sometimes under the guise of farmer versus banker, is a hostility which often overflows into the political arena. The businessman, and others in the private sector, sneer at the public servant with his supposedly comfortable and secure position, and at the unions for causing the economic downturns in the country, while the unionists say it's the greedy monopolistic capitalists who are at fault. There is a law for those who are not rich, where there is no presumption of innocence. There are many more examples to add to this state of confusion—and confusion it is, but classless it certainly is not.

Social Class & Status

For real wealth and real power in Canada, inherit it, or marry it, or forget it.

Walter Stewart,
The Wealthy Canadians, 1976

Take the public library, for instance. The Westmount Public Library is for Westmount people, nobody else. In order to get a card you must prove residence, and you do this with a letter from either your bank manager or a Westmount property owner.

Robert Fulford, 1967

For those who cannot attain the great wealth of a Thomson, Irving or Taylor, there are positions which will bring money and a chance to live the good life, in the proper environment. It seems natural for them to band together in protective ghettos—British Properties in Vancouver, Rosedale and Forest Hill Village in Toronto, and Westmount in Montreal. The name "Westmount" has symbolized the perfect Residential community for those who have made their money and are secure in their social prominence.

Robert Fulford, 1967

It is wrong to say that Canadians have no distinctive national characteristics; what about our national custom of Keeping Down with the Joneses? In other countries people keep up with the Joneses; they vie with one another in the acquirement of showy and prestige-giving possessions.... It is only when he goes on a holiday to the U.S.A. that he splurges, takes suites in hotels, gives huge tips to hirelings and drinks pearls dissolved in wine. At home he likes the neighbours to think that he is just keeping out of jail.
Robertson Davies in Marchbank Almanac, *1967*

The Canadian taxpayer is a very docile and passive creature with a somewhat dull appearance but looks great mounted...
Times Colonist, *January 11, 2004*

We ain't the Waldorf-Astoria. If we were, you wouldn't be here. You ain't Pierpont Morgan. If you were, you wouldn't be here. We know this hotel is on a bum. What about yourself?
Frank Rasky, Journalist, 1975

Canadians are as class conscious a lot as anyone else, although we, along with our American neighbours to the south would never admit it.
Anon., 2006

Land-a-mercy, we are smug. We are smugger than a Baptist preacher with his hands on the keys to every liquor closet and chastity belt in town.
Walter Stewart, 1976

Economics

Tory times are hard times.
Anon., Liberal Party adherents' claim since 1930s

No matter how often the politicians may proclaim that Canada's economic system spreads abundance among the many, in reality it creates wealth for the few.
              Peter C. Newman, 1975

The day is going to come when people are going to say, "Why were you so stupid? Why did you give it all away?"
                Eric Kierans, 1973

It is difficult to generate much enthusiasm for buying Canadian stocks.
           The Financial Post, *December 29, 1984*

The financier was visiting a doctor for his annual check-up.
"Well, Doctor, how am I?" he asked.
"You're sound as a dollar!"
"American or Canadian?" he asked cautiously.
                Robert Shelly, 1976

The effect on Ontario Industry and Tourism Minister Frank Miller after his partners explained how business was done in Quebec.:
"It scared the hell out of me and I came back here to Ontario."
          The Globe and Mail, *December 3, 1984*

Canada joined the large collection of countries that keep pushing ahead of them a heavy National Debt; all the best countries have unredeemable national debts.
                 A.R.M. Lower,
             Colony to Nation, *1946*

One thing everybody agreed on, however, is that if you live in Canada and you have at least $1.00 in your pocket you probably buy tickets once a month, if not once a week.
           The Financial Post, *December 29, 1984*

Canada has not had a voice of authority for years. We have provided a happy hunting ground for people with money, seeking people with businesses to sell, who were selling to make a tax-free capital gain. Since 1929, when Mckenzie King and C.D. Howe called the plays, the hunting has been very successful, with no interference by anyone because it was supposed to be investment money.

Walter H. Hamilton, 1968

I'm disturbed because the doctors tell me I'm as sound as a dollar.

John Diefenbaker, 1975

Take the petroleum industry: Canada's Imperial Oil poses as an old Canadian firm, and to most of us the word "imperial" suggests that British tradition. Actually, Imperial was taken over by Standard Oil...back in 1898.

Andrew Manorie, 1976

I know of no money-making business in Canada except the Law, Store Keeping, Tavern Keeping, and perhaps I might add horse dealing.

John Langton, in a letter to his brother,
October 21, 1884

Business men, where are your voices today? In 1911 you spoke. But today you are silent while things are done which you know are wrong. You watch this government going along the road to socialism. Is it that, fearing you will be called cap-in-hand to the throne of Bureaucracy, you seek to protect yourselves with your silence? If so, you will only tighten the bands that still bind you.

John Diefenbaker, 1948 speech to
P.C. Businessmen's Club, Toronto

Yankee go home—but not until you've spent all your money.

Sign on fence in Winnipeg

We have no interest in Canadair, de Havilland or anything else the Canadian Government has managed to screw up, and you can quote me on that.
Douglas Reekie, 1984

We dig up our resources for Americans. We manufacture for Americans. Now we even sell to ourselves...for American store owners.
Andrew Manorie, 1976

No more are Marc Lalonde jokes heard across the land (Q: How do you get a small business in Canada? A: Get a big one, and wait).
Red Deer Advocate, *1985*

Banks

Compared to the English bank, a Canadian bank is as informal as a potlatch. Not until he enters a London branch of Barclays or the Royal Bank does a Canadian realize that banking is a solemn rite to which the client is slightly less vital than the teller's thumb sponge.
Eric Nicol, *from* Shall we Join the Ladies?, *1972*

Along with *Anne of Green Gables*, Calgary red eye and Casa Loma, the Canadian banking system rates right up there among great Canadian accomplishments.
A Concise Dictionary of Canadianisms, *1973*

Calgary red eye, a mixture of tomato juice and beer, a drink associated with Calgary, Alberta, and the surrounding area [since] 1964
The Globe and Mail, *Toronto, October 16, 1973*

I don't know why Canadians are upset about bank profits. We stopped screwing Canadians. Now we are screwing foreigners.
Bank of Nova Scotia Executive,
November, 1981

James Sayers, Secretary, Trust Companies Association of Canada:
"Well, no, tricycle going up against a steam roller, I don't call that competition."
Walter Stewart, 1982

It looks pretty complicated when you peek in the door, says a man who has worked for the Royal for nearly three decades, (but it isn't). You look it up, follow the rules, or you won't last long. This is strictly a paint-by-numbers business.
Walter Stewart, 1982

The Law

I never laughed so hard as I did when I read the headline about the police designing handcuffs for the elderly. In a city with a rampant drug trade, notorious sex industry and petty theft, it gives me great confidence to find the department has expended time and money trying to figure out how to contain obviously the most violent of all criminals, the elderly.

Are the police officers going to have to ask for the "criminal's" age before they decide which cuffs to use?
Jesse Williams, Oak Bay.
Times Colonist, *June 13, 2007*

Impaired:
A drunk driving charge. Used both as a noun and an adjective. Street-talk equivalent, "pissed to the gills."
Graham Hicks, 2004

Yes, well there are a lot of bleeding hearts around who just don't like to see people with helmets and guns. All I can say is, go on and bleed, but it is more important to keep law and order in this society than to be worried about weak-kneed people...

*Pierre Trudeau, addressing
the Press Club in Washington,
D.C., March 25, 1969*

The Americans come up here and admire us for the way we hang criminals. They sit in our club and say, "You certainly do hang them, don't you!" My! They like to hang a few! The day may be coming when they will. Meantime, we like to hang people to make the Americans sit up.

*Stephen Leacock, "I'll Stay in Canada,"
in* Canadian Anthology, *ed. C.F. Klinck
and R.E. Watters, 1955*

This bylaw is the pits:
Sitting by a campfire on the open range, strumming your guitar and cooking up a pot of beans with your trusty horse at your side, gazing at the stars—ah, those were the days. Today, that romantic western lifestyle has morphed into the backyard fire pit, up to 40,000 which exist in Calgary.

Backyard fires have become so popular that city hall wants a bylaw to impose stricter rules for fire safety, including moving pits farther away from houses and making people douse their fires at midnight. Surely, this is not the cowboy way. This here's the West, dang it anyway, where personal freedoms are cherished and a man ought to be able to have a fire on his own back 40 if he wants.

Calgary Herald, *2004*

Law firms want me on their letterhead. And they pay me one hundred thousand dollars a year just to hang around. But that's not the way I want to go out.

John Diefenbaker, 1971

If British Columbia wants to be taken seriously back East, maybe we should stop looking like a bunch of tree-hugging granola-eating gurus.

Bob P. Nicholas, Times Colonist,
Victoria, 2004

Peaceful law-abiding people:
All I knew about Canada was from geographical and historical lessons at school. Then I remembered a poem by Seume which we had to recite at school, entitled "The Savage". It described how an honest Canadian red-skin was tricked by a white trader and the Indian repaid evil with good.

The Possibilities of Canada
are Truly Great! Memoirs 1906–1924
by Martin Nordegg

In short, for most Canadians charged with criminal offences the unrich, the unlettered, the un-well-connected—there is no presumption of innocence.

Walter Stewart, 1976

The B.C. justice system is rather like an old Laundromat. Its wheels grind slowly. It makes strange, sloshing noises. And it's generally as soft as washing.

Jon Ferry, The Province,
January 28, 2004

Criminal Convictions:
No sooner does the merit of an article establish its success with the public than the brood of imitators who live on other peoples' reputations are after it with their counterfeits.

Messrs. LEA & PERRINS have recently obtained criminal convictions against several parties in Montreal and Toronto for refilling their sauce bottles with some mawkish decoctions.

Saturday Night, *August, 1893*

Canadian civil liberties, in short, are just as much in danger from the left as the right, and just as likely to be undermined by smugness and neglect as by tyranny. In times of calmness and tranquility, we have nothing to worry about. But as soon as the going gets rough, our liberties go up like a lift-bridge, and we are subjected to exactly the same kinds of hassles as other peoples elsewhere in countries whose lack of freedom causes us to shake our heads in regretful sympathy. Our freedom of speech is subject to recall, free assembly depends upon with whom we want to assemble, and even freedom of thought is subject to seasonal variations.

Walter Stewart, 1976

I'm a musician too, I have a degree. You can buy a wig.

*Gerald Levey, Vancouver Magistrate,
to Franklin Hamilton, guitarist, on ordering him
to have his hair cut, December, 1966*

Changing Values:
All over the country there are cases of young men being ordered by the courts to get their hair cut. Canadian Press reported from Montreal that same fall: "Judge J. Redmond Roche made it clear that young men with shoulder-length hair have two strikes against them when they appear in court before him." The judge, who already knew the answer, had just asked a youth if he were a man or a girl, and when the defendant replied that he was a man, the judge snapped that he didn't agree with him and gave him a summary ten days in jail on a shoplifting charge.

Pierre Burton, 1968.

The Foreign Connection

An Australian observer, passing through, notes that Canadians are sprung from the peasant class of Britain.

Archibald MacMechan, 1974

If we have to pick a dance partner, I say let's drop the gloves with the Danes. We could dazzle 'em with some fancy Latin mottos, and they could draw a cartoon of Stephen Harper with a bomb for a hat, sparking riots in Calgary.
Jack Knox, March 12, 2006

Living next to you is in some ways like sleeping with an elephant. No matter how friendly or even-tempered is the beast, if I can call it that, one is affected by every twitch and grunt.
Pierre Elliott Trudeau, 1969

U.S. presidential hopeful Barack Obama, already under fire from fellow Democratic candidates for his supposed inexperience and unguarded comments on American foreign-policy issues, is raising eyebrows again after vowing to call "the president of Canada" if elected to the White House to begin renegotiating terms of the NAFTA trade deal.
Randy Boswell, CanWest News Service,
Times Colonist, August 9, 2007

I have just taken the most shameful oath of my life, sworn allegiance to the Queen of England.
David Ouelette, 1962

Canadian-American Behaviour:
Canada is the greatest country under the Stars and Stripes.
James A. MacDonald, editor,
Toronto Globe, Speech in Massey Hall
to Assoc. Clubs of America, 1914

Hugh Ess:
The Mare Can nation. So convenient as the Hugh Ess has been to the development of the Canajan ethos that if the Hugh Ess did not exist it would be necessary to invent it.
Mark M. Orkin in Canajan, eh?, *1973*

Americanization:
You are a big country now, but you still tend to feel small and fragile. If the U.S. gets a cold, you get pneumonia.

Herman Khan, 1972

Say, you jolly Canucks, how do you like the prospect of becoming hewers of pulp wood and drawers of water power for the Americans?

Eye Opener, *September 16, 1911*

There really is no anti-Americanism here as far as I can see. The American business manager can go to the golf club or anywhere else. Some people actually look up to the guy: They think he must know more because he's an American. It's a curious Canadian hang-up.

Max Saltsman, 1971

At least three American holidays have been adopted in Canada—Arbor Day, Labor Day and Thanksgiving Day—and Decoration Day has been transplanted in a measure. Labor Day is celebrated on the same date in Canada as in the United States, and an agitation in favour of adopting the American date for Thanksgiving probably had been successful but for the fact that it is too late in the season to suit Canadian climatic conditions.

Samuel E. Moffett, 1972

The historian A.R.M. Lower said, "Canada is a supreme act of faith."

"Canada is the only country in the world that knows how to live without an identity," suggested Marshall McLuhan.

Interviewed in Buenos Aires, the Argentine writer Jorge Luis Borges noted, "Canada is so far away it hardly exists."

John Robert Colombo, 1983

Does any sane, sober-thinking Canadian doubt for a moment that it is only the British flag that prevents the aggressive and greedy nation to the south of us from stripping us to the bone of all desirable territory?

Ottawa Citizen, 1903

All over the world people are laughing at Canada chasing after Mao and saying, "Won't you allow us to recognize you?" I can just hear the Secretary of State for External Affairs [Mitchell Sharp] saying, "Here I am, Mao, take me."

John Diefenbaker, 1969

Trudeau has cut a dash, but other nations often think Canadian politics boring. Canadian complacency about their political purity abroad and security at home has lead to the phrase, "Ugly American, smugly Canadian."

Jeannette Harris, 1976

The Prime Minister spoke in Halifax on October 22 and said, "There is a continuing dialogue going on between the United States and Canada." ...Dialogue. When they went down there a high official, speaking of the Canadian idea that was presented, said, "Their ideas are screwy."

John Diefenbaker, 1963

One of the problems we face as a nation, perhaps in greater measure than other nations, is that we are held captive by the myth of the reasonable citizen. The Canadian as we see him, the Canadian in the mind of God, is a man who never gives in to extremism; he is a patient man (who shuns violence), a neighbourly man (who spurns racism), a democratic man (who supports free speech, civil liberties, and honesty in politics). He is, in short, all the things your average wild-eyed, gun-toting, bigoted, loud-mouthed, venal, aggressive, tyrannical bastard of an American is not.

Walter Stewart, 1976

CANADIANS: SERIOUSLY HUMOROUS

To get a mention down in Washington, you have to be either Wayne Gretzky or a good snowstorm.
Brian Mulroney, 1985

The Easygoing Canadian:
A political convention in the United States bears the same relation to a political convention in Canada as bedlam bears to a cemetery.
J. MacCormac,
Canada: America's Problem, 1940

"By jove," the Britisher exclaimed, "Why do you blokes close your drinking establishments on today of all days? I wouldn't imagine anyone could vote for any of those candidates sober!"
A visitor from the United Kingdom, paying his first visit to Canada on election day, 1976

Canadians seem to be happier than Americans. At least they're more contented and more balanced. They don't hemorrhage if an order is slow getting out and, after all, they argue, is one late order worth an ulcer?
American's comments, 1963

The people back home consider you as someone who went away and deserted them. We're just as Canadian even though we are not living at home. Canadian in feeling...you've got to face facts. There is a tendency to small thinking back in Canada."
Monty Hall in Raymond Reed's
The Canadian Style, 1973

BBC Executive Michael Smithson, explaining why European broadcasters are urging caution in allowing cable television—a rush of American commercial programs —to take over the industry:
We don't want to become like Canada.
The Red Deer Advocate, May 18, 1984

I trust I shall not be presumptuous when I state that I verily believe that the militia of Kentucky are alone competent to place Montreal and Upper Canada at your feet.

Henry Clay, 1850

Quebec, at least for an American, is certainly a very peculiar place.

Benjamin Silliman, 1822

"If the United States should accept us as their new State, they would do so on certain conditions and in accepting these, we would have to crawl on our knees. Canadians are a proud nation," he states.

Robert Bonner, 1966

Suddenly he declares: "The best way for Canada to fight the American influence would be for all of us to speak French only."

Pierre Berton, 1966

CANADIANS: SERIOUSLY HUMOROUS

The Environment

A WELL-KNOWN AXIOM of the Australian outback, which applies to Canada as well, is "If it moves, shoot it; if it doesn't, chop it down." Unlike the First Nations peoples and the Inuit, who took care to preserve their environment, the white man has raped and ravished virtually every corner of the land in which he plunders into, in his lust for fortune from the soil, either through agricultural or mining pursuits. As a result, Canada has endured, and is losing, a terrible battle since the white man first stepped foot on its soil. The ravages of the onslaught are to be seen throughout the land.

The tide may be turning at last as awareness and concern about global warming and pollution come to the forefront of our minds. Business and government are finally, albeit reluctantly, getting into the act, and that may stay the hand of the desecrators from further acts of willful destruction of our world's natural beauty. Serious pollution problems will have to be dealt with soon, or there will be little left of this country to shoot or chop down.

Pollution

The enormity of the water pollution problem came home to me this past summer when I had occasion to be out for a walk on Lake Erie. I met a young woman who lived nearby who claimed that she had been taking the Pill with water out of the lake. The next time she was in to see her doctor, he informed her that she was three months stagnant.

Dave Broadfoot, 1974

Bill Davis and Drew Lewis, the two men named to "take a hold of the problem" of acid rain at last month's Shamrock Summit, met for the first time Friday, and said later they agreed to "lay plans to establish an approach to an agenda" for future talks.

The Edmonton Journal
April 20, 1985

In 1985 acid rain in Canada's lakes will be solved by throwing in "massive doses of Rolaids."

Brian Flynn, Peterborough, Ontario,
Member of the Rhinoceros Party,
The Red Deer Advocate, *January 4, 1985*

The flush toilet cheats the land and pollutes the rivers.

Miriam Chapin, 1959

One much appreciated and unexpected benefit of the snowstorm and subsequent below-zero freeze up of our local lotus land has been the deafening silence of the usually vocal environmental lobby on the subject of global warming. Makes me warm all over!

Bill Davis, Victoria,
Times Colonist, *November 29, 2006*

Fresh Air

Canadians hate air.

Frances Monck, 1891

The time will soon be here when my grandchild will long for the cry of a loon, the flash of a salmon, the whisper of spruce needles, or the screech of an eagle. But he will not make friends with any of these creatures and when his heart aches with longing he will curse me. Have I done all to keep the air fresh? Have I cared enough about the water? Have I left the eagle to soar in freedom? Have I done everything I could to earn my grandchild's fondness?

Chief Dan George

CANADIANS: SERIOUSLY HUMOROUS

You Call that Culture?

MANY CRITICS WOULD dispute that a section devoted to culture should be included in this work since those who believe that such a measure of civilization is of no use in describing Canada. However, as the term culture is one of the most protean words in the English language, we can be excused for its inclusion.

In describing the culture or customs of a society, we can broadly include any unusual practices, habits, or conventions which are characteristic of that society, and that is what we have done.

Within that rather liberal definition of culture then, we may include a collection of quotations which brings to a higher level of consciousness an awareness of a culture, of sorts, emerging through the cracks of a frontier society.

Culture (General)

Most Canadians are people between 0 and 100, who build their body and soul with a steady diet of cardboard toast and American television.

Stefan Randstrom,
The Globe and Mail, *July 1, 2004*

It wasn't a big shout—I'm Canadian.

Gordon Pinsent explains his reaction to the news that he would get the Award of Excellence at the Banff International Television Festival, 2004

Canada is a country with two official languages and no official culture.

John Robert Colombo, 1975

The English-speaking Canadians protest that they will never become Americans—they are already Americans without knowing it.

Samuel E. Moffett, 1972

There is no galvanizing a corpse! Canada is dead—dead church, dead commerce, dead people. A poor priest-ridden, politician-ridden, doctor-ridden, lawyer-ridden land. No energy, no enterprise, no snap.

Toronto Leader, *April 28, 1870*

You know, it's no wonder Canadians are having an identity crisis! The other night, I decided not to watch American television. Instead, I jumped into my Volvo, drove down to the local Chinese restaurant, ordered a pizza, then went to an Italian Western and got back home just in time to watch a re-run of the Russians beating us in hockey.

Robert Shelly, 1976

I just can't imagine anyone thinking even for a minute that Canadians are dull. Isn't our favourite colour brown?

Jack Tennant, 1985

A Canadian is someone who drinks Brazilian coffee from an English teacup, and munches a French pastry while sitting on his Danish furniture, having just come home from an Italian movie in his German car. He picks up his Japanese pen and writes to his Member of Parliament to complain about the American takeover of the Canadian publishing business.

Maclean's, *April, 1973*

The Canadian Flat Earth Society will hold its annual picnic and horizon-scoffing contest on Sunday. It will be held near the north edge.

The Farceburg Gazette in
The Air Farce Book, *1980*

Do Canadians work? Very few.

Conscious that the way to beat inflation was to encourage restraint, the Canadian government set up a committee. The finding of this committee was published in 1975. They discovered that an unemployed person used more restraint and spent less money than he did when he was employed. Since this discovery, the government has persuaded as many people as possible to leave their jobs. The program has enjoyed a tremendous success.

Ben Wicks, 1976

85

Mary Kelly, an American reviewer, describing *The Valley of Doubt*, a movie about a young American girl in the Canadian Northwoods:
"In casting, a successful effort has been made to select a variety of racial types such as would naturally be found in surroundings as remote and sparsely settled as these. There's a certain crudeness of feature and manner that belongs to such characters and this the director has not lost sight of. The presence of conventional folk from the city only further emphasizes this quality."

Pierre Berton, 1920

You grow up eating Kellogg's Corn Flakes and driving Chevrolet cars, and you know all the good things in your life come from somewhere else. So you think the place to go for ideas is where the Corn Flakes came from.

Leslie Armour, 1971

When Canada's fledgling movie industry was just getting started, film budgets were very small. Penny-pinching and belt-cinching became de rigueur. It led one producer to hire a native Indian to predict the weather, thus saving money by not scheduling any shooting on those days the Indian predicted inclement weather. The cost was high, but worth it. And for two weeks it worked. When the Indian said it was going to rain, it rained. When he said it would be clear, it was clear. But then one day the Indian didn't submit his prediction. The producer visited the Indian.

"You've done very well for us, predicting the weather perfectly. Why is it today you can't tell us the weather?"

"Radio broke," the Indian explained.

Robert Shelly, 1976

If one were restricted to a single word to describe Hollywood's image of Canada, that word would be "primitive."

Pierre Berton, 1975

Steve Penfold would likely consider the gooey Boston Cream doughnut a quintessential definer of Canadian social identity. The cream-filled doughnut with chocolate icing has an American name, it belongs to a confectionery brand that is an American fixture, and yet it is one of the perennial top sellers at Tim Hortons stores across Canada and is embraced by Canadians everywhere as "their" doughnut.

"It is the classic story of Canadian economic history and Canadian cultural history to make what is not Canadian Canadian. We are a culture that borrows," says Dr. Penfold, a history professor at the University of Toronto.

Anne Marie Owens,
The National Post, January 3, 2004

Health

Health:
All aid short of help.

Harold Wilson, qu. by Blair Frazor in
The Listener, March 1953

Lady at [a] soldiers' convalescent hospital: "Where were you wounded, young man?"

Newman (leg propped up and wrapped in a quarter-mile of bandages): "I was 'it in the head, ma'am, but the bandage slipped."

Red Newman of The Dumbbells,
Post World War I Theatrical Reviews

Graffiti:
FIFTY-EIGHT PERCENT OF ALL DEATHS ARE FATAL.

Another Specimen of Graffiti from
the students of Pauline Johnson Collegiate,
Brantford, Ontario, 1973

If Canada has as many physically ill as there are mentally ill, the government would declare a national emergency.

Donald Sinclair, 1963

After medicare, what is next on the womb-to-tomb welfare list? Well, there are legal care, morticare, carcare, housecare, leisurecare, and endless other possibilities.

Lubor Zink,
Toronto Telegram, *July 26, 1965*

Home Remedies for Bugs:
Being once troubled with bugs, I know how to sympathize with anyone who has them. I have tried various cures but to no avail when one day my daughter came in and said, "Mother, your troubles are over. I have a cure for bed bugs." The cure was gasoline. So I bought two gallons. I gave my bedsteads, mattresses and every place where I thought they could get a good soaking twice. The gasoline hurts nothing, if you keep it away from fire. Be very careful of a blaze, or you will rue ever having used it, for it is very inflammable.

Well, I used the gasoline in this way five years ago, and I have never seen a bug since.

Grain Growers Guide, *Circa, 1915*

Labour

Canadians don't riot, for pete's sake; it's uncanadian!

Walter Stewart, 1976

Labour Strikes:
　Bloody Saturday.

Winnipeg General Strike, *June 21, 1919,*
when men died and injury
and damage were widespread.

Education

No country but a country of alienated mad men would hire 75% of its professors in one year from outside the country.
A Canadian Professor, 1972

The future is not what it used to be.
Donald Johnston, 1984

Universities:
For God's sake, can't you find me a suitable Canadian to teach Canadian government?
John Holmes, 1968

Academics:
And we watch come out in their twos and threes the
professors of the humanities,
Well-fed, half-drunk from their formal dinner,
Old phonies all, each a miserable sinner.
And I can't help smiling—are these, are these
The ones who are touted as "our enemies"?
Raymond Shouster, 1958

Architecture:
I believe it will take a thousand years to develop a national style in Canada, but I do see a light in the west over a grain elevator.
Eric Authur, 1928

The Language

Eh?
Rhymes with hay. The great Canajan monosyllable and shibboleth, "eh?", is all things to all men.
Mark M. Orkin in Canajan, eh?, *1973*

Charles Dickens was the first to use the term "polar bear," reports Britain's *Daily Express* newspaper. Before him, it was called "white bear."

Michael Kersterton, "Social Studies,"
The Globe and Mail, July 1, 2005

Bourassa was also unready to guarantee education in the language of the parent's choice, and an Atlantic parent complained: "I feel like a bridegroom who had finally decided to go to the altar with the girl who's been asking you for years to do the right thing by her, and when I turned 'round to put the ring on her finger, she'd gone.

Atlantic Delegate at the Victoria
Conference, February, 1971

Bilingualism

"I am sorry I have never been able to learn the French language, so as to make a speech in French. I do not have an ear for sound. I am like the Leader of the Opposition [Robert Stanfield] who has a capacity of intonation which I lack. But I would remind you, Mr. Speaker, that the Right Hon. W. L. Mackenzie King, who was my member for years, only made two speeches in French in his entire life. Once he said 'Oui' and the second time he said 'Oui, oui.'"

John Diefenbaker, 1973

To demonstrate how simple it is to learn the language of La Belle Province, here is a brief glossary of familiar French words and phrases:
 coup de grace . . . . . . mow the lawn.
 Tête a tête . . . . . . my bra is too tight.
 Peu . . . . . . that's really strong cheese!

Robert Shelley, 1976

The insistent, and to say the least, wholehearted method, by which a certain section of French-Canadians of the Province of Quebec hope to maintain the supremacy of the French language in that section of Canada is ridiculous if nothing else.

Saturday Night, May 1909

The shotgun marriage between French and English-speaking Canada has become a marriage of convenience. Hopefully a divorce won't ensue.

Jeanette Harris, 1976

Where did this hooey come from about two founding races, the English and the French? I suppose the strong aspirations of 6 million French in Quebec—but only as I would, for 6 million Scotsmen, if there were such a group huddled together in the Maritimes, or 6 million Ukrainians if such was the make-up of the prairies.

Brian A. Brown, 1978

French Language

Jean-Guy wants to know if you know why the electric light switches in Quebec say "ON" and "OFF" only in English. Because, he says, "we French know when de light is off."

Robert Shelley, 1976

I have often said that the great problem for French Canadians is that there are no French Canadians.

Abbé Lionel Groulx, 1936

Montreal is the only place where a good French accent isn't a social asset.

Brendan Behan, 1983

It is customary to divide the Canajan population into Francophone and Anglophone. On the French Canajan side the fishle language is French, used for statutes, classics, scholarly journals and the things that nobody bothers to read. Most French Canajans, while they read and write French, talk Joual, the nash null language of Quebec. It is not necessary to teach Joual since every native son already speaks it. Besides, no manuals of instruction exist. Why should they?

Mark M. Orkin in
Canajan eh?, 1973

I wrote a letter to Premier Bourassa enquiring about Bill 22. I asked if he could explain it to me. He replied in French, explaining Bill 22 in detail. I don't understand French, but I understand his reply perfectly.

A Quebec Anglophone, 1977

English Language

Without a working knowledge of English, any man on any street corner in any town or city in North America is a dead duck.

Walter H. Hamilton, 1968

We hire twenty outstanding graduates each at Ford [Motor Company of Canada] and find they cannot make a simple report in basic English.

William Bourke, 1963

In Canada we have enough to do keeping up with two spoken languages without trying to invent slang, so we just go right ahead and use English for literature, Scotch for sermons, and American for conversations.

Stephen B. Leacock, 1943

Sex

They have sex in Canada?

Ringo Wilde,
Times Colonist, 2003

Regarding our sexual powers, he asks, "How do most Canadians regard sex?" and answers, "as a blank on an application form."

Bill Mann

But Canada is a lover that one will never bed.

Andy Wainwright, 1969

...the Canadian lover has no understanding of a woman's unquenchable need for Dalliance. He fully expects to pop in during the afternoon for a few hours, make love, have a few words about the state of his business affairs, grab a cup of coffee, and run off to the next appointment, leaving his mistress feeling unsatisfied and slightly chilled, even though the love-making interlude included a rare orgasm."

Joan Finnigan
(writing as Michelle Bedard),
Canada in Bed, 1969

Of what use are my hands
if you won't let them caress you
My arms, if they can't embrace you?
Oh my whole frame's
become a piece of useless junk...

The season that lovers
and worms wait for
is here...

Irving Layton, 1971

Thirty-four percent of all adolescents agree that having sex together is a good way for two people to become acquainted.

The Montreal Star, February 20, 1973

A Canadian is someone who knows how to make love in a canoe.

Pierre Burton, 1975

Who knows whether or not Allan Fotheringham was right in 1976 when he wrote:
The key to understanding Alberta is androgen, the male sex hormone, and the aura it projects, the insecurities it hides, the locker-room mentality it bolsters, explains the new right kid on the block—the province of cowboys and nouveau-riche swagger.

John Robert Colombo, 1983

And from Gudgeon's studies, is there a unique Canadian sex move or position or excuse not to?
Yes, there is. I think the quintessential Canadian position is woman on top, man in the next room.

Dan Murphy, 2003

Food and Drink

Why are wild salmon turning up covered in sea lice? Wild salmon taste better.

Times Colonist, Victoria, 2004

Then there was the guy who walked into a restaurant in Montreal and asked for a salad with French dressing. He got a plate of lettuce, a slice of tomato, grated cheese, Bermuda onions and a picture of Premier Robert Bourassa putting on his pants.

Robert Shelley, 1976

Maybe we're the mad ones.

So, we keep animals in cramped, filthy conditions, grind up other, usually sick animals and put the resulting soylent green into their feed, then top it all off with mega-doses of antibiotics to keep the wretches more or less alive so they can eventually stagger to the slaughterhouse. Then we whine because they're diseased and we're going to catch whatever it is they have because we ate them.

Well, I think we're the ones who are mad, not the cows.

F.M. Vandale,
Times Colonist, Victoria,
January 10, 2004

Of all people in the world, I think the Canadians, when drunk, are the most disagreeable for excessive drinking generally causes them to quarrel and fight among themselves. Indeed, I had rather have fifty drunken Indians in the fort than five than drunken Canadians.

Daniel W. Harmon,
Journal, December 25, 1802

In Canada we have tried everything to keep the winter chill off, from coffee to coats, but the best is still booze.

Anon.

Beware of Bootleggin':
Your short article on home brewing ("Starting Post", Sept. 1, 1982), omitted an important fact: One must have a license from the Department of National Revenue, Customs and Excise Division, before undertaking home brewing. A license fee is not required, but approval of an application may take many weeks. Also, it is illegal to offer or give any homemade beer to anyone other than a family member who resides with the person making the beer. Your friends cannot enjoy your beer, according to the government.

Dr. K. Barry Heath, Kindersley, Saskatchewan,
"Letters," The Financial Post Magazine,
October 15, 1982

CANADIANS: SERIOUSLY HUMOROUS

Robert Chambers Edwards published the *Eye Opener* in which he attacked almost every abuse including drink though he himself gazed at the world through a fog of whiskey fumes. His favourite and oft-printed prayer began: "Lord, let me keep a straight way in the path of honour and a straight face in the presence of solemn asses."

Bob Edwards, August 4, 1906

At any rate, prohibition has made Alberta safe for hypocrisy.

Eye Opener, September 3, 1919

Indians also know, from long experience, that excessive drinking annoys white people. It gets them upset. They pay attention to a drunken Indian; a sober Indian they never see. Drinking is an excellent way for the Indian to get Canadian attention.

Heather Robertson, 1970

This report that whiskey drinking is declining in Calgary will cause no surprise. Most of the politicians are out of town telling the festive farmer which way to vote.

Eye Opener, September 2, 1905

A restaurant in Alberta displays a sign advertising "Real Texas-style Alberta fried chicken." Only in Canada, you say.

Anon.

Jason Gileno, director of the hockey documentary *The Chiefs*, on filming in Laval, Quebec:
"We ate a lot of poutine and Tim Hortons food. It was a very Canadian experience."

Times Colonist, March 20, 2005

Saanich Councillor Bob Gillespie, calling for a cull of Canada geese in the Sooke reservoir: "We should open up a new café in town and sell goose burgers."

Times Colonist, March 21, 2005

Art and Literature

The bald truth is that Canada has the money, but would rather spend it on whiskey than on books.

Robert Barr, in Can. Mag., *November 1899*

To Canadian literature I have given more time and labour than it deserves. Canadians are mainly barbarians and consist, ninety-nine out of one hundred, of backs and stomachs. To expect our polished boors to enjoy art in any of its developments is too much.

Charles Mair, 1891

Painful self-criticism as opposed to defensive self-deprecation has never been a very important feature of Canadian life.

Donald Cameron,
Faces of Leacock, 1967

What would happen in Canada if full sovereignty were invoked and the southern border was sealed tight against American mass culture—if the airways were jammed, if all our comic books were embargoed, if only the purist and most uplifting of American cultural commodities were allowed entry? Native industries would take over, obviously. Cut off from the American junk, Canada would have to produce her own.

Richard H. Robere, American reporter,
in Maclean's, *November 1960*

Support your fellow Canadians. We should buy lousy Canadian novels instead of importing lousy American novels.

Johnny Wayne,
Toronto Star Week, *April 20, 1968*

CANADIANS: SERIOUSLY HUMOROUS

Canadians don't buy Canadian books. And if they won't, who will? It's a proven fact.

Anon., 1954

People put down Canadian literature and ask us why there isn't a Moby Dick. The reason there isn't a Moby Dick is that if a Canadian did a Moby Dick, it would be done from the point of view of the whale. Nobody ever thought of that.

Margaret Atwood, 1972

Quebec libre, hell! Quebec broke! Without my Ontario market I couldn't survive.

Anon.,
French Canadian Artists, 1972

The great Canadian patriotic songs of the Second World War were, "There'll Always Be An England," and "The White Cliffs of Dover."

Raymond Reid, 1973

Will nobody write a few songs for Canada?

Thomas MacQueen, 1867

No dead Canadian poet has had any influence at all.

Milton Wilson, 1959

The first qualification of the student of Canadian literature is a thick skin. He must be incapable of being bored.

Kildare Dobbs, 1958

Poetry in Canada is at a discount. Epic, dramatic, lyric, spasmodic, it is a drug, a very asafetida [devil's dung or stinking gum] pill, in the literacy market. The publisher keeps it at arms length; then turns up its nose at it. It has no exchange value at all.

John Reade, 1872

A critic who discovers a flaw in Canadian literature is considered very clever; but the critic who discovers genius in our poetry or prose is immediately taunted with nationalistic prejudice.

Wilson MacDonald, 1931

Has Canada no poet to describe the glories of his parent land—no painter that can delineate her matchless scenery of land and wave? Are her children dumb and blind, that they leave to strangers the task of singing her praise?

Susanna Moodie,
Mark Hurdlestone, 1853

A Canadian poet is a man who gets snowed on.

Elizabeth Rodriguez, 1970

Ottawa Art:
Ottawa doesn't know its arts from a hole in the ground.

Anon., quoted in
Canadian Annual Review, *1968*

The cold narrow minds, the confined ideas, the by-gone prejudices of this society are hardly conceivable, books there are none, no music, and as to pictures!—the Lord delivered us from such! The people do not know what a picture is.

Anna Jameson,
on Societies in Toronto, 1837

"Well," the struggling young artist was telling a friend, "the Canada Arts Council finally accepted some of my work. And they liked it so much they hung it right outside their office."
"Really? What was it titled?"
"Ring bell and walk in."

Robert Shelley, 1976

Our artists are like troops sent ashore to establish and hold vital bridgeheads, endlessly promised reinforcements, endlessly denied them.
Who will drive this home to those whose responsibility it is to ensure the intellectual health of the country? It is time to differentiate between unproductive myths and functional reality.

Tom Hendry, 1984

In the art of architecture we have no recorded names worthy to stand with Michelangelo and Christopher Wren.

Bruce Hutchinson in
Canada Tomorrow's Giant, 1957

Gerry Eldred, Executive Director of the Stratford Festival, explains the festival's rising deficit:
"Last year, the problem was one of over-spending, whereas this year, the problem is one of under-budgeting."

The Globe and Mail,
December 6, 1984

Probably the ugliest building in Canada of its size and cost is the new Parliament House and to obtain this when on the neck of nature, this deformity on the face of the park, this ill-begotten piece of architecture, the Ontario government went abroad. It would be absurd to say that we have no architects, for handsomer buildings have been built since the Parliament Buildings were begun. It is equally untrue that we are without sculptors.

Saturday Night, *May, 1892*

Lorne Michaels, the University of Toronto alumnus who created *Saturday Night Live*, once told a panel that Canadians would never had made a movie called *It's a Wonderful Life*—our version would have been *It's an All Right Life*.

Peggy Curran,
CanWest News Services, 2006

YOU CALL THAT CULTURE?

A famous English poet, who was somewhat disillusioned about Canada, once wrote:
The only poet in Canada was very nice to me in Ottawa. Canada's a bloody place for a sensitive real poet like this to live all his life in.

Rupert Brooke

You know our Emmys are like your Geminis, but sharper. I cut myself on them. They're quite dangerous, and oddly enough, allowed on planes.

Jon Stewart,
Daily Show *host*

Miscellaneous

We've created a society in which, if you touch another person, you apologize.

Richard J. Needham,
Coca-Cola, 1969

Canada Contact:
Canada, alas, is forgetting that it is its pioneers who built this country and made it what it was; now it wants to be like everyone else and have autocamps instead of human beings.

Malcolm Lowry, 1950

I move about in Canadian circles to some extent and I hear nothing but bad reports of all the men I look up to in Canadian life. There must be a very wicked set, but I must confess that Canadians speak as badly of the men in private life.
Canada is a village street, many thousands of miles long.

Lord Beaverbrook,
letter July 4, 1917

Canada is a secondary and second-rate country without much depth of experience: everyone admits that—too freely sometimes.

A.R.M. Lower in
Canadian History Review, *1941, 12*

On one of their visits to Canada, the Royal family joined in Vancouver's celebration of British Columbia's 100th birthday. At one function, hundreds of children clustered to cheer their presence.

"Where did all these children come from?" the Queen asked, with cheery surprise. "Oh," a local politician answered absentmindedly, "we've been preparing for this day for several years."

Robert Shelly, 1976

Off-the-record remark which appeared in Canadian newspapers, referring to Canadian attitude:

Inject in the picture the "get-your-man" slogan, and...it is fairly certain the feature will have strong audience appeal.

Matthew A. Taylor,
in Moving Picture World, *1921*

Canadians do not queue (or "line-up" as they say in Canada) for a bus. They much prefer to conduct themselves in an animal-like manner and elbow their way past those of smaller stature.

Ben Wicks, 1976

Marriage and Divorce:
The English rule prohibiting marriage with a deceased sister formerly prevailed in Canada.

Samuel E. Moffett, 1972

A few years ago, somebody asked Mort Sahl what he thought of a country that didn't even have a national flag.

"Well," he said, "it's a start."

Lister Sinclair, 1979

To make mistakes. As in the Canajan proverb: to err is yoomin, toofer give duhvine.

Mark M. Orkin in Canajan, eh?, *1973*

A fisherman was trying his luck on a wharf when another man happened by.

"How many fish have you caught?" he asked.

"Well," the angler replied, "if I catch the one I'm after and three more, I'll have four."

Anon.

CANADIANS: SERIOUSLY HUMOROUS

For the Love of Sports

FROM THE TIME our early ancestors first whacked a rock with a stick, we have been engaged in a love affair with sports. Hit a rock across ground—you've got field hockey. Hit it through the air, you've invented baseball. Run with it, you've got football, kick it you've got soccer. Whack it over a frozen lake and you've started one of Canada's great passions—ice hockey.

Those who don't play either crowd the bleachers or gather in front of their television sets to cheer their teams. If the national pastime isn't playing sports, its knowing all the player stats, bemoaning trades, and knowing how a particular play should have been made. Just as blistering hot days and wide blue skies give rise to games of scrub baseball, so the frozen lakes and ponds of our great country beckon young and old to suit up, don skates, and sail across the ice. Viva la sport!

Sports (General)

Violence in Lacrosse:
If a lacrosse player fails to agree with the ruling of the referee, he not only disputes the point, but upon occasion proceeds to "eat up" the said official with his fists. . . . He gets off with a reprimand, to assault someone else later on ...

Saturday Night, *August, 1911*

Olympic Games (Montreal, 1976):
The Olympics can no more have a deficit than a man can have a baby.

Jean Drapeau, *1975*

Calgary–Edmonton sports rivalry:
I hope the rivalry never ends! It's great! I just wish we would beat 'em in something one year!

Tom Forzani, *1985.*

The Wave:
It's time to scrap this ridiculous ritual which features people in sporting arena stands standing up, sitting down, spilling beer and blocking the other fans' view of the game!

The Calgary Sunday Sun, *December 30, 1984*

How do you force 300 Canadians out of a swimming pool?
Say: "Would everyone please get out of the pool?"

Times Colonist, July 16, 2006

I shudder to think what would have happened to the World War II effort if we had depended on track and swimming participants instead of mannish hockey players.

Stan Obodiac, 1970

The playpen: term used to describe the world of professional sport.

Dick Beddoes, Sports Editor,
Toronto, Globe and Mail,

The New Seven Wonders of the World were announced this week. "Just missing the cut at No. 8," says Toronto comedian Frenchie McFarlane, "was the Maple Leafs winning the Stanley Cup. No. 9 was our under-20 soccer team scoring a goal."

CanWest News Service,
Edmonton Journal, July 15, 2007

Golf

Golf is the favourite game in Scotland. It is played everywhere. It is too slow a game, however, for Canada. We would go to sleep over it.

John B. MacLean, 1891

Hey fellas, lets have a golf weekend. We could easily make it into a family sport. Why can't your wife and children be used as caddies and ball finders?

Hugh Johanson, 2001

There is a sign standing on a golf course in Nova Scotia that states:
> GOLFERS WILL PLEASE REFRAIN FROM PICKING UP LOST BALLS UNTIL THEY HAVE STOPPED ROLLING.

I made half a million, but I spent a million. Gawd, it used to drive me crazy.
George Knudson, 1985

Golfers are more gentle than usual on those golf courses. Men who use the foulest language everywhere else suddenly use expressions like, "Oh, great putt," "bad luck," or "nice try" when they miss a one-foot putt.
Cliff Kelly, 2004

Football

During an unusually spirited football game between two rival CFL teams, the referee called a clipping penalty and walked off fifteen yards. As he did so, a player yelled out, "You stink!"

Without a pause, the referee stepped off another fifteen yards, and called back, "How do I smell from here?"
Robert Shelley, 1976

Harold Ballard, incurred the wrath of certain members of his Tiger-Cats when he referred to them as "a bunch of overpaid bums." One player who was upset with the comment was Zambiasi, Hamilton's middle linebacker.

"I think," said Zambiasi, "maybe Ballard got his hockey and football teams mixed up."

Ballard, of course, also owns the Toronto Maple Leafs.
The Calgary Sun, December 26, 1984

Wouldn't want to suggest Saskatchewan Roughriders fans got a tad ahead of themselves after last Sunday's big win over Edmonton, but WestJet reported a sharp increase in the number of callers inquiring if banjos are allowed as overhead luggage on flights to Ottawa.

National Post, November 15, 2004

Baseball

It is no trivial matter that baseball is becoming the national game of Canada instead of cricket. It has a very deep significance, as has the fact that the native game of lacrosse is not able to hold its own against the southern intruder.

Samuel E. Moffett, 1972

Why is it that Jarry Park has so many exits? Do you know what you're saying? Obviously you haven't seen these guys play?

A Montreal Expos baseball fan

Hockey

It was the strangest goal I've ever seen. I didn't see it."

*Bob Johnson, "the Badger,"
coach of the Calgary Flames, 1984*

If the Prime Minister ever again says Canadians lack confidence, I'll give him a kick in the pants.

*Conn Smythe, in a television interview,
May 3, 1967, after Toronto Maple Leafs
won the Stanley Cup*

The NHL ship is so tightly organized that even the robber barons of old couldn't have devised a more monopolistic feudal setup.

Nick Auf Der Maur, 1971

Gordie Howe, hockey player and commentator:
"All pro athletes are bilingual. They speak English and profanity."

*Lisa Wojna,
in* Canadian Quotes, *2005*

Don Cherry is not amused. A British newspaper rattled the hockey attack dog's cage by putting his beloved game on its list of top 10 overrated things in sport.

"Is it a coincidence that the country which produced the inexplicably popular Celine Dion should also have come up with a sport that is almost unwatchable?" writes Alasdair Reid in the London *Sunday Times*.

Cherry was ready to drop the gloves.

"Any people that have a sport like cricket, where they stop for tea halfway through the game wouldn't understand a good man's game like hockey," Cherry said.

Reid continued: "If you actually see the puck you might see the point, but it zips across the ice invisible to the naked eye, the whirling antics of men wrapped in bedspreads the only clue to its whereabouts."

Cherry didn't hesitate to hit back: "Anybody that plays sports in short pants, what can you expect?"

Gerry Axelsen, 2004

The men get wildly excited about it. But...if the players get over keen and lose their tempers as they are apt to do, the possession of the stick and the close proximity to one another gives the occasion for many a nasty hit.

*Lady Aberdeen,
describing hockey, 1894*

Organized hockey brings out the best in young boys and the worst in some parents according to a group of "hockey mothers" from Etobicoke... Each has seen or heard of mothers physically attacking coaches and shouting obscenities at players...
"The women are more vicious than the men. You just have to look at their faces in the stands," said Betty Moffatt of Tallon Rd.
"It's difficult to keep calm when a mother yells at her son to 'get' your son," she said. "No wonder some mothers turn around and haul off at each other."
The Toronto Star, January 24, 1972

We have several rivalries that border on mayhem.
Brian O'Neill, NHL Director of
"Crime and Punishment" in the
Calgary Herald, January 12, 1985

Whether it's a hornets' nest or not, there's a lot of honey to be found in a hornets' nest.
Rick St. Croix, Toronto Goaltender,
in The Globe and Mail, December 13, 1984

Toronto Maple Leafs: Team motto: "Winning isn't everything!" The Leafs are sometimes erroneously referred to as the "Maple Laffs," but that would suggest a certain entertainment value. Famous for not quite winning.
Will Ferguson and Ian Ferguson,
How To Be A Canadian, 2007

How close is Toronto to a good hockey team? About three hundred and seventy-five miles if you go by the 401 and don't miss the Montreal cut-off.
What's the difference between the Maple Leafs and a skunk? The skunk's colours are black and white.
The Toronto Star, December 7, 1984

CANADIANS: SERIOUSLY HUMOROUS

Toronto Maple Leaf owner Harold Ballard on the work ethic of his hapless hockey team:
You can't be a hockey player and be some kind of pansy.
         The Globe and Mail, *December 5, 1984*

You can't lick 'em on the ice if you can't lick 'em in the alley.
         Remark attributed to Conn Smythe

It's an unwritten rule in hockey that fighters fight and guys who don't want to fight don't. "You don't see a fighter fighting a non-fighter," Wayne [Gretzky] says. "When a fight breaks out on the ice, "I always look for Pierre Larouche, Thomas Gradin, Neal Broten —all the little guys I can grab."
         The Globe and Mail, *1985*

Hockey is a religion here. We're all priests. It's sacred. You don't trade priests.
         Guy Lafleur, 1985

Odds & Ends and Leftovers

IN THIS SECTION I have included quotations which do not appear to fit into any of the preceding sections in the book, but which are congruent with the preceding sections, in that they enlighten us further about Canada and her people. I understand that many of the subheadings with only a single quote may be best included in this category. However, I did not begin this work by formulating headings and subheadings and then searching for quotes that fit into those categories. I decided to research humorous put-downs about Canada and Canadians, thus allowing me to ascertain just where the humour lies in Canada and Canadians. If a category has only one or two quotes in it, then maybe that aspect of Canada and her people, places and things lacks humour, or perhaps I just couldn't find it.

Odds & Ends

How do you get a Canadian to apologize?
Step on his toes.
Times Colonist, July 16, 2006

Automobiles:
  The trouble is that too often there is forty horsepower under the bonnet and one asspower at the wheel.
John MacNaughton, D.D.,
Calvin, Que., Queen's Court, 1933

The souvenir Anne of Green Gables shot-glass for sale in Prince Edward Island: I must have missed that episode.
Brent Butt, Times Colonist,
November 4, 2006

While Banting, a Canadian, is rightly remembered for insulin, the maker of syrup, a still more improbable discovery, lies in some unmarked grave beside the St. Lawrence. History is seldom just.
Bruce Hutchison in
Canada, Tomorrow's Giant, 1957

Aca nada" or "Nothing of value here!"
First Spanish sailors on failing to find gold in Canada

It was my first encounter with a grizzly. I met many afterwards. I never found one that would attack. I always had trouble to get near enough for shooting. They always ran away.

> The Possibilities of Canada
> are Truly Great! Memoirs 1906–1924
> by Martin Nordegg

...the old saying is: You give them a millimetre, and they've taken a kilometre."

> Alberta Transportation Minister
> Marvin Moore, in the Legislature,
> November 23, 1984

Snow is still worse, because, besides the dampness from melting, it lowers the temperature of the body, and the teeth chatter.

> The Possibilities of Canada
> are Truly Great! Memoirs 1906–1924
> by Martin Nordegg

What do you call an Albertan in a suit? The accused. What do you call a British Columbian in a suit? The deceased.

> Jack Knox,
> Times Colonist, January 16, 2005

Leftovers

He must be Canadian.
He knows nothing about Canada.

> Calgary taxi driver, 1985

Canadian Destiny:
  A Canadian is someone who knows he is going somewhere, but isn't sure where.

> W. L. Morton, 1965

Nevertheless, it's fair to say that Canadian humour, like Canadians themselves, is self-deprecating, aiming squarely at anyone who seems to think too highly of himself—often an American—or anyone else who doesn't, usually a Canadian.

Peggy Curran,
Times Colonist, *July 16, 2006*

Quando Omni Flunkus Moritati (When all else fails, play dead.)
Motto of The Red Green Show

Canada is the perpetual wallflower that stands on the edge of the hall, waiting for someone to come and ask her for a dance. A fire breaks out, she risks life and limb to rescue her fellow dancegoers, and suffers serious injuries. But when the hall is repaired and the dancing resumes, there is Canada, the wallflower still, while those she once helped Glamorously cavort across the floor, blithely neglecting her yet again.

That is the price Canada pays for sharing the North American continent with the United States , and for being a selfless friend of Britain in two global conflicts.

Kevin Myers,
The Sunday Telegraph, *London, 2008*

Enough. Canadians, as a people, are no better and no worse than anyone else.

Walter Stewart, 1976

ISBN 1425147151